D1493318

AN INTRODUCTION
TO MILITARY GEOGRAPHY

AN INTRODUCTION TO
MILITARY GEOGRAPHY

BY

BRIGADIER-GENERAL E. S. MAY, C.B., C.M.G.

GENERAL STAFF IRISH COMMAND

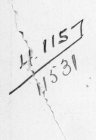

WITH MAPS AND SKETCHES

LONDON
HUGH REES, Ltd.
119, PALL MALL, S.W.
1909

PREFACE

SOME two years ago I published a little book called "Geography in Relation to War." Small as it was, I am assured that my effort was of some slight service, and I have been asked by many interested in military education to write a fuller volume.

Urged by these representations, I began to add to my original venture, but circumstances have prevented me from carrying out my project, and I have not covered nearly so wide a field as I had intended. I am informed, however, that what I have already put together will be of use, and I am therefore publishing what I can only call an introduction to the subject I had hoped to deal with more adequately.

My thanks are due to Colonel C. B. Mayne, late Royal Engineers, for some valuable suggestions. Dr. Martin and Major-General Rochfort, C.B., have kindly looked over the proof of the chapter on Abyssinia. General Sir Edwin Collen, G.C.I.E., has done me a similar service in respect to the chapter on Afghanistan and the North-West Frontier of India. Mr. F. Hudleston has kindly verified some references for me. To the many others whose works I have consulted, I hope I have given due acknowledgment in my text.

Nowadays, when the intimate relationship between politics and strategy is so thoroughly understood, it is, I hope, not necessary for me to explain why I have sometimes dwelt on certain aspects of geography not always associated with the commonly accepted meaning of that term.

EDWARD S. MAY.

DUBLIN,
November, 1908.

CONTENTS

CHAPTER I

WHY OFFICERS SHOULD STUDY GEOGRAPHY

CHAPTER II

ARTIFICIAL AND NATURAL FRONTIERS

CONTENTS

CHAPTER III

Some European Frontiers

CHAPTER IV

The Influences of Geographical Features on Operations

CHAPTER V

THE SEA IN RELATION TO OPERATIONS OF WAR

CHAPTER VI

LINES OF COMMUNICATION

CHAPTER VII

CANALS AND WATER-WAYS

CONTENTS

CHAPTER VIII

STRATEGICAL RAILWAYS IN PROCESS OF CONSTRUCTION

CHAPTER IX

PERSIA

CHAPTER X

Afghanistan and the North-West Frontier of India

CHAPTER XI

ABYSSINIA

CHAPTER XII

MANCHURIA

CHAPTER XIII

Conclusion

LIST OF MAPS

AN INTRODUCTION
TO MILITARY GEOGRAPHY

CHAPTER I

WHY OFFICERS SHOULD STUDY GEOGRAPHY

THE term Geography is connected with so many sciences, and has so many ramifications ; there are so many factors involved in the successful conduct of large military operations ; so many influences are at work, or have been at work, in shaping the destiny of nations—that it is difficult to decide where some branches of geography may or may not be legitimately discussed in connection with military inquiry. Properly speaking, we should begin by giving a geological basis to our studies. Before the history of war comes the history of man, and before the history of man the story of the evolution of the territories he inhabits. Much interest would be aroused, and time not wasted, were we to investigate back, and still farther back, until we approached the realm which, for want of a better term, is known as Chaos, where the forces of Nature wrestled and fought together, the resultant of their Titanic energies, exhibited in upheavals and subsidences, being the world in which we live to-day.

1

Physical geography comes obviously in sequence
to geology, for this latter science deals with the
forces that have shaped the progress of the world;
the traces of their handiwork are to be discovered
in the broad avenues of approach which they have
formed for the migration of pristine races, or, again,
in the high mountains that they have piled to block
such movements.   Military, succeeding physical
geography, is also rooted, therefore, in geology,
and certain strategical axioms of to-day are based
on conditions established when the world was
young.   Nor need we stray beyond our own islands
for an illustration.   " The structural slope of Britain
inward towards Europe is an expression of growth
from the Northern Atlantis.   The whole recent
history of mankind would have been different were
the landward angle of England divided from the
Continent by a channel rifted through uplands."[1]
We have, in fact, grown from south-eastern roots.

India was intended by Nature to be detached
from Central Asia, for India is a plateau of ancient
crystalline rock once wholly detached from the
main structure of Asia, though the channel has
silted up, and is now represented by the alluvial
deposits along the feet of the Himalayas and the
Suleiman range.   There is, therefore, a geological
foundation for the strategical efforts we have made
to block an inroad from Central Asia.   How the
distribution of land and water on the surface of
the globe has affected winds and rainfall, and
how these in turn have influenced climatic con-

---

[1] *Britain and the British Seas*, by H. J. Mackinder, M.A., second
edition ; Oxford, at the Clarendon Press, p. 353.

ditions, and therefore the development of races, is sufficiently obvious; even more easily recognizable are influences such as the existence of fresh water, humidity of the air, and retention of water by the soil. The relationship between the geological structure and the shape of mountains is expressed in the trend of water-partings; these in turn govern the scheme of the rivers, and in studying the military geography of a country we cannot do better than follow up the path of its great watercourses. We are soon in touch with questions of vegetation, of crops, of the distribution of domestic animals, with villages, towns, great cities, fortresses. We reach them by *communications*, and the story of a nation's struggles and growth hinges upon these. For communications govern supply, and supply governs war. In a word, the most casual inquirer must perceive how absorbing are investigations as to cause and effect in operation before the features of nature were modified by man. In these crowded days, however, we are obliged often to take things as we find them, and to touch but very lightly on geology.

Physical geography, however, must always form the basis of geography in general. In itself we have been accustomed to regard it as a dry science, perhaps because of the manner in which it was presented to us when we were young. In our schooldays the majority of us learnt by rote the definition of an isthmus, an island, a peninsula, and so on, the names of the principal rivers in the various countries and the heights of their loftiest hills, with, perhaps, a list of their products and manufactures in addition. Plain facts, unflavoured with any application to real life, formed our daily fare. We were not taught in a way to make us think, as Jowett once hoped we might have been, and therefore we were soon wearied, and forgot geography as quickly as we could.

THE INFLUENCE OF GEOGRAPHY

During recent years, however, owing largely to the exertions of the Royal Geographical and similar societies, and the work of Professor Mackinder, and other writers of distinction, a new state of things has arisen. The influences of geography, direct and indirect, on mankind and on the doings of mankind, have aroused growing interest; and now everybody recognizes that all, or almost all, sciences are in some way or other under obligations to or connected with geography. Thus history, botany, zoology, and the art of war, have all become closely associated with it. But all these ramifications of the influence of geography spring from that science which treats of the condition of the earth's surface as it now exists, including the distribution over it of mankind, of animals, of various products, of the natural phenomena of its different regions, and of how they have been conditioned by artificial agencies.

It will be well to begin by pointing out the general nature, object, and importance of military geography, by showing how closely this subject should be studied by officers, and how intimately connected it is with strategical and tactical operations. But a wider field than that of physical geography alone must be traversed. Military geography regards the geographical features of the earth with a view to military operations; but man has modified the original condition of the ground, and therefore wherever armies meet topography has to be considered, and the artificial details of a country prove often as important as those of natural origin.

Further, in an empire such as ours, strategy and warlike operations on a large scale must almost always embrace considerations affecting the operations of both army and navy; and therefore, when we study military geography, we have to devote considerable attention to the sea, that portion of the globe which many former writers on the subject used barely to mention.

Tactically considered, of course, the sea has less interest for us in a geographical sense than the land. The sea has been said to be all one. It is certainly so in its strategical aspect, which implies that no limit and no narrow confines can be set to sea-power; but tactically it is all one in a more restricted sense, in so far that the combatants who meet upon it fight upon a level arena the same in every respect for both, and where no advantage is to be gained by a clever use of the features of the theatre of combat. In selecting a commander for a certain enterprise, it is no little recommendation that he should know the country. It is no small advantage to a general that he can utilize the peculiarities of the terrain to hamper an opponent strange to the region; but no admiral would be selected because he knew a particular water, for the simple reason that fleets never engage but with ample room beneath their keels, and that it is no part of naval tactics to utilize shoals or rocks to the discomfiture of an opponent—coast defence, of course, being left out of sight for the moment.

It may be thought that it is hardly necessary to dwell long on the necessity for officers studying military geography as it has here been defined, especially officers of our army, whose duty calls them to so many different portions of the globe.

To say that the nature of the country must influence operations is to assert what all will recognize as a mere truism. Interest in the subject will be enhanced, however, if the principal directions in which such influence may be expected to make itself felt are recalled to mind.

ESTABLISHMENT OF BASES

In the first place, let us consider the establishment of a base of operations. In the case of oversea expeditions this will mean a seaport. To rapidly seize a seaport implies surprise. We must usually try and snatch it by a *coup de main*, because such havens are usually fortified, and if war be imminent we may assume that their defenders will be on the alert. We may very often, or even usually, therefore, have to throw a force ashore on an open beach, and by a rapid raid from such a precarious foothold gain possession of a better one by attacking a harbour on the land side.

The depth of water, the direction of the prevailing winds, the presence of surf, the set of the tides, the character of the beach, the existence or otherwise of a position from which the disembarkation may be covered, the avenues of approach inland, the water-supply and facilities for camping—all these considerations have on such an occasion to be closely examined, and they, one and all, are connected with military geography. For an oversea expedition, then, at the very outset, a knowledge of the military geography of the country to be assailed is essential.

But in many parts of the world our frontiers are coterminous with those of potential enemies. We may in such regions wish to establish a land base, and in that case we shall find that a knowledge of military geography will again be of immense assistance. The security of the base from any enterprise on the part of the enemy, the existence of routes from it by which provisions and stores may be conveyed to and distributed along the line of communications of the fighting force, the best positions for the establishment of posts for securing those communications, for depots, for hospitals, and for all the other necessities of an army, have to be thought of. Rivers and canals, hills, roads, railways, firewood, must all be kept in view, and every one of these is included within the sphere of military geography.

COMPOSITION OF ARMIES, AND ESTABLISHMENT OF LINES OF COMMUNICATION

A knowledge of the nature of the country where operations are to take place will teach us how our army must be organized; whether it is to be strong in mounted infantry, whether cavalry are likely to find an opportunity for their special characteristics, whether artillery can turn its long range to account, whether pack or wheeled transport will be necessary—all these questions are governed by a knowledge of the military geography of the country, and the general who leaves them out of sight will fare badly. If his knowledge of the country will enable him to look beyond his base and immediate advance, he will be able to perceive where the directions of columns may be changed, where, in all probability, they may most suitably unite, where a change of base and communications may be established, or how the original channels of communication can be improved.

RESOURCES OF THE COUNTRY OPERATED IN

Further, not only the nature, but the resources of the theatre of war will have to be studied. Is it fertile, or otherwise? What districts will supply most food and forage? Where can cattle and horses be found? Is the climate such as will render the provision of tents necessary? Is the winter so severe that roads may be blocked by snow, or lakes and rivers rendered passable by ice? Above all, is there a rainy season which may destroy or impair roads and create mud?—mud which Napoleon, remembering Poland, designated "the fifth element" (J'ai trouvé en Pologne un cinquième élément : c'est la boue ").

It is with resources—food, fuel, and forage—that a general is perhaps most concerned. In the days of comparatively small armies the productions of the country operated in were of immense importance, because they could contribute very largely to the support of the troops. Supplies nowadays, when enormous armies engage, and when, owing to long-ranging and rapid-firing weapons, and a higher standard of civilization, more ammunition, more medical comforts, more food, and more technical stores, have to be carried, become the dominating factor and the most difficult problem in warfare. It is popularly supposed that the art of war consists in destroying life ; it would be more correct to describe it as the art of sustaining existence. If we want to kill our enemies, we must enable our men to live, and it is the inability to find food that has frequently caused the overthrow of the most powerful armies. In 1674, when Sobieski, with five to one against him, freed his country from the Turkish menace, it was hunger imposed upon the enemy, and not destruction of life, that gave him the victory. The horses of the Turks died and their cavalry were dismounted. Their guns had to be abandoned. Their best officers succumbed to the effects of privation. At last the invader of Poland was glad to retire with the remnants of a shattered army to the banks of the Danube. Yet the Turk is the most frugal of soldiers, and, as has been said, soldiers were hardened to less liberal treatment in those days than they are now.

A lack of supplies in a devastated country forced Massena to retire from the lines of Torres Vedras. It was the attempt to feed the Russian armies by a single line of rail that protracted the war of 1877-78. Most salient example of all, it was an inhospitable country and a rigorous climate, reinforcing the Russians in their destruction of the French magazines, that annihilated Napoleon's hosts in 1812.

Valuable as the resources of a country may be, to live on them an army must move forward and a war be carried out without lull or respite. When armies pause in their stride, the country close to them is quickly exhausted, and they must rely on magazines or depots of provisions prepared in rear of the columns. Even in so rich a country as France, the Germans, in 1870, found that only one-third of their supplies could be gathered by requisition from the territories they traversed. It is significant that even as far back as those days 3,000,000 pounds of preserved provisions were ordered from England at the beginning of hostilities.

Forage, perhaps, is the greatest difficulty of all, because, in the first place, it is bulky ; and, secondly, because the animals that draw supplies have themselves to be fed, and every animal eats as much in weight of grain alone as three or four men. The larger the supply train, therefore, the heavier the call upon it. The greater the provision the

more inexorable the demand, unless we fight
in regions where mechanical transport may help
us out; but that too, it should be remembered,
requires the establishment of depôts for fuel and
repair.

In practice we become forced to look to the
country wherein we are to operate for a large
proportion of forage. We must therefore be
closely acquainted with its productiveness and
with the various descriptions of food-stuffs which it
grows. We must not be satisfied with information
derived from one year only, but we must compare
the records of several seasons, and must be prepared to meet bad harvests, if such vicissitudes are
probable. We must also know what the chief
pursuits of the inhabitants are, whether agricultural
or commercial, whether they live by tillage of the
soil or by grazing animals, whether they measure
wealth in terms of bushels or oxen.

Such are some of the considerations that the
mention of resources raises in our minds, but to
British officers there are others besides. The sea
is at once our strongest ally and our servant. Our
ultimate base of supply is the world. Hay from
Russia, oats from Canada, meat from Australia,
coffee and tea from our Indian Empire, mules from
Spain, and horses from Argentina—all are borne
across the ocean, as long as we retain command of it,
to preserve the fighting energy of our men and the
mobility of our armies. British officers, therefore,
should not only be acquainted with the resources
of countries in which it is possible, or perhaps
probable, that operations may take place, but they

ought to be familiar with the products of every region of the globe, so that in time of stress we may supply our armies, not from or through England only, but direct from any distant country which will give us what we want.

Our contracts would then be carried out at a cheaper rate than if we had to make them at home, and the supply to our troops in the field would be more rapid than in the case of a country which must supply her armies from her own resources. While, therefore, a platitude may have been uttered when it was asserted that the resources of a country in which operations are likely to take place must be studied, none is involved when it is pointed out that the resources of all countries should be familiar to British officers, and that an extensive know-ledge of an important branch of geography is absolutely essential to those staff-officers whose duties may some day call them to arrange for a supply by sea of such commodities as an army needs.

As regards other characteristics, Europe, thanks to the works of foreign geographers, is now fairly accurately known by many. Dr. Miller Maguire in this country (to whom the writer is indebted for many hints) has written ably on military geography, too. Thanks to the industry of such men as Niox, Marga, Lavallée, Dubois, and Camille Guy, to mention but a few, the main features of those countries in which they have been interested can be studied. It is not probable that mistakes which were made a hundred years ago, when the Black Forest was regarded as terrible and

impenetrable as the haunted forests of the old
romancists, will be repeated. It is as little likely
that a Napoleon will again regard Bohemia as a
region of mountains as that some unborn Shake-
speare will make a drama hinge on adventures near
its sea-coast.[1] But officers who have not had
opportunities of travelling may scarcely even now
appreciate how greatly customs in various European
countries vary from one another and differ from our
own. Oxen, and even cows, are still to be seen
drawing the plough in certain places within easy
reach of England. Waggons primitive in construction, and but little different from the " buck
waggons " of South Africa, are still to be found.
The progress of civilization has been accompanied
by deterioration amongst certain races in certain
countries—as, for example, amongst the Mussulmans
of Bosnia-Herzegovina, who have become greatly
addicted to strong drink—rather than by the progress
which we might have expected. The variations of
climate, and their effects, too, will always offer an
immense field for research. The rainfall and phenomena connected with it must not be overlooked.
A British force may, again, be placed in jeopardy,
just as, during the Peninsular War, Hill was
isolated by the rapid swelling of the Nive on
the night of December 12, 1813, and Beresford
was exposed to the attack of Soult through the
sudden flooding of the Garonne during the night
of April 3 of the next year. We should remember
how the same French Marshal's divisions, marching
to the relief of St. Sebastian, found themselves in

[1] *The Winter's Tale.*

difficulties when heavy rain rendered impassable the fords of the Bidassoa behind them.

SOUTH AFRICAN EXPERIENCES

But all foreign territories in which we may have to operate have not been so closely studied as Europe.

We can most of us remember incidents in South Africa when rivers which were found to be absolutely dry on one day formed raging and impassable torrents a few days later. We can call to mind dongas where our enemies took shelter, to be swept away by the sudden flooding of a thunder-storm. We do not forget that springs and ponds were looked for in vain at the end of a day's march, because there were no surveys to consult, and intelligence proved inaccurate. We recollect occasions when fords were sought to no purpose by the attacking column which was to use them, and we remember the useless labour of our opponents at Ladysmith trying to make an artificial flood under protest from the natural features of the ground.

Why renew again accursed records of catastrophe ? Enough has been said to show that a thorough knowledge of the country in which he is going to operate is a considerable recommendation in a general ; and where other qualifications are equal, it may well prove decisive when choice is made. To know the military geography of the country in which they happen to find themselves, and where, in the case of troops abroad at any rate, they may at any moment have to fight, should, however, be the duty of all officers. Indeed, the monotony of service during peace-time might well be varied by exercises which would embrace the study of the country in the neighbourhood of cantonments, and such tasks would attract the interest, and foster the powers of observation, of those told off to undertake them, far more than work possibly as scientific, but certainly more abstract in character.

STUDY OF NEIGHBOURING DISTRICTS BY OFFICERS IN PEACE-TIME

Matters are very widely different now to what they were previously to the South African War, and reconnaissance work receives much attention. It is not probable that we shall ever again be at a loss as we often were during the last Boer War, even when operating in our own territories. Since those days we do not trust to fortune, and have improved on a time when the only available map of Ladysmith and its environs, which enormously assisted us during the siege, was one executed before the war for his amusement by Major Grieve, of the Royal Artillery. In this connection, officers commanding our units may find encouragement in the example of that fine old veteran, still happily with us, Count Häselar,[1] the late commander of the army corps in Metz, who, in view of eventualities, studied the ground in the vicinity of that fortress with an assiduity to which the walls of his study bore silent testimony, for they were papered with maps of the surrounding district.

---

[1] He has died since these words were written.

WEATHER

While in the preceding pages the influence of the ground has been dwelt on at length, comparatively little has been said as to weather ; and yet weather and climate and seasons are essentially geographical phenomena, and directly affect military operations perhaps more than any other of the ramifications of that science.

The influence of rain or thaw is obvious, and has been touched upon. The conditions of the climate which may or may not bring them about should be carefully studied and known. When the soil is a foot deep in mud, assaults can scarcely be impetuous, artillery and cavalry move with difficulty, and combats are less decisive in their issues, as rapidity of pursuit is impossible.

The seasons of the year affect tactics also. The greater part of the work of war can only be accomplished in the daytime. To win decisive battles prolonged hours of light are necessary. A few hours added to a day will make the difference between a mere defeat and an annihilating rout. Since the sun stood still for Joshua many a triumphant commander has prayed for a lengthened evening. On the other hand, night has come to the rescue of not a few clinging desperately to safety. "Night or Blücher !" is as apocryphal as many traditions, but our enemies in South Africa did often fight for the night. The coming of darkness may be deliberately counted on to break off an engagement, and for that reason a reconnaissance in force should only be commenced in the late afternoon. In winter, marches are more irksome, not only on account of snow and mud and ice, but because cold affects the vigour of men and saps their energies. The start in the early morning is more difficult, and the day is curtailed at the other end. Warm food is more indispensable ; cold produces hunger and makes other heavy calls on the transport and supply columns or on the health of the men.

Other phenomena connected with weather will affect the progress of battles. The haze that in early morning often hangs over river valleys during autumn may greatly modify operations. We remember the meadows watered by the Meuse shrouded in grey mist on September 1, 1870— the morning of Sedan. The soldiers struggling blindly in the November fog at Inkermann are not yet forgotten. Mist and rain—and stupidity— nearly lost us Albuera. Such are some experiences. They might be added to by illustrations from the German operations during the Le Mans campaign, when frequently a thick morning mist lying over the snow-clad fields disastrously shortened the working hours of war. Baron Von der Goltz[1] tells us how difficult it is, under such circumstances, to drive an obstinate enemy out of a country which is advantageous to him. The engagements began late, the advance of the firing lines were impeded by snow, the early evening put an end to fighting just as the disintegration of the enemy's lines showed success to be within reach. The length of

[1] *A Nation in Arms,* by Lieutenant-General Baron Von der Goltz. London : Hugh Rees, Ltd., 1906, p. 394.

the winter's night, too, made it possible for him to rally again, to occupy fresh positions, to receive reinforcements, and gather himself together for renewed resistance on the morrow. The process of destruction which was being wrought in the French army was so frequently interrupted that it lost its force. The Germans, had the season been summer, would have completed in three or four days what, in winter, cost them seven to accomplish. Delay, too, reduced results by half, for in war rapidity multiplies success. The same author points out that, among the causes which led to the loss of the Battle of Kunersdorf, the great heat protracted during a long summer day must be reckoned. But if the season did not favour Frederick at Kunersdorf, it was kind to Zieten at Torgau, for it was the coming darkness which enabled that leader to take and hold the heights of Stiptitz. The duration of daylight is certainly a factor to be reckoned with when a battle can be prearranged.

It is scarcely necessary to point out how much the health of troops is affected by unfavourable or trying weather, disastrously so when want of supplies is added to its inclemency. Our own annals bring this home to us in the story of the Walcheren Expedition, and more recently of the Crimea. But it was felt even by the successful Germans in 1870, and especially so during the siege of Belfort. Such considerations lead us to reflect how much sanitation and questions of health must be studied in relation to geographical conditions. The campaign of 1870, when the great issues were decided in summer, and in an extraordinarily rich and highly populated country, cost the Germans 400,000 sick. The average duration of the absence of a sick man from his regiment may be taken at twenty days. What the fighting efficiency of an army suffers by its tally of men in hospital can easily be calculated. The climate and degree of civilization—that is to say, the geographical conditions—of the land in which war is waged will modify and influence the sanitary measures that we must take. Obviously, a war in the East or in tropical climates demands quite different preparations to those for a campaign in Europe.

It is not only the health and alimentation of man that must be studied : certain regions of the world have characteristics highly inimical to the life and health of horses, which foresight and careful inquiry must endeavour to meet. Sand-colic, for example, may annihilate a cavalry brigade for all practical purposes in a few days. Horse sickness is a real danger. The tsetse-fly may deny whole districts to mounted troops.

But the illustration of a well-established truth needs no further elaboration.

CHAPTER II

ARTIFICIAL AND NATURAL FRONTIERS

Frontiers are a salient example of the value of a thorough knowledge of military geography on the part of those who direct imperial strategy. Artificial frontiers can never equal those dictated by Nature as revealed by geography, although the spread or ambitions or necessities of particular races and accidental circumstances have in many cases fixed the boundaries of States, and have set Nature at defiance. A very interesting example is to be found in the peculiar manner in which the Russian frontier is pushed northwards into the Finmarken, leaving a little spit of Russian territory in the country of her neighbour. The causes of such eccentricities must be read in history, or may be left to speculation; it is enough to say here that symmetry has not invariably been studied where boundaries have been drawn. Nature herself has not, however, always been able to give security with frontiers. Mountains are but a feeble barrier. The Pyrenees have often been passed. We know that the huge tumbled mass of mountains on the north-west frontier of India guarantees no absolute security to us. During the late Russo-Japanese war we have seen great armies traversing mountains and rivers that seemed a little while ago to constitute impassable obstacles. In truth, to set a formal limit to enterprise and military ardour is a hopeless task. We can no more find security in the possession of so-called "keys" or behind natural features than we can behind continuous fortifications such as the Great Wall of China. That was in the mind of Lord Beaconsfield when, in the House of Lords, he made his famous paradox, and said: "The key of India is in London!" Whatever might be the exact boundary which scientific men should trace thousands of miles away, the sway of empire, while London was London, would be ours. While London retained its pre-eminence, while London stood for the energy and courage of the race, and represented the wealth and resources of the British Empire, no reverse on a frontier far away would shake England from her determination to hold her own.

But, while deprecating any pedantic reliance on natural advantages, it must surely occur to us that a better understanding of geography on the part of statesmen and leaders of public opinion would often have prevented some hideous misconceptions and blunders affecting seriously in the future strategical operations.

Frontier questions, in fact, cause perhaps our greatest anxieties. Once we may be said to have had one frontier—the sea. To-day our condition is that of a continental nation, considering the Empire as a whole and the world as one continent. No other nation has such a stretch of territorial frontier to defend and safeguard ; no other Government is confronted with such a variety of difficulties.   In North America our territories march with those of the United States for more than 3,000 miles.   In Africa we are called upon to watch 12,000 miles, constituting frontiers with France, Germany, Italy, Portugal, and the Congo State.   In India we have to deal with the most troublesome frontiers of all, although their extent is not half as great as in Africa, for our possessions march with those of Persia, Russia, Afghanistan, Tibet, China, Siam, and France.[1]   The responsibilities on land of the greatest Sea-Power overtop those of any other Power in the world.

How many great national complications, how many possible causes of war, have not arisen from ignorance of military geography on the part of those who drew or assisted to draw the frontier line !   We all remember the dispute with the United States, recently happily settled, as to the frontier line between British Columbia and the territory of the United States in Alaska—a legacy of the Russo-English Treaty of 1825—and the carelessness as to terms of geographical definition which brought about the long wrangle.   Neither have we forgotten the dispute as to the frontier line of Venezuela, or the disastrous consequences that might have been its outcome.   We can most of us recall the tension that existed when what is known as the Penjdeh crisis was upon us in the year 1885.   The disputes which circled round the question of a scientific frontier for

[1] Romanes Lecture by Lord Curzon, November 2, 1907.

India in the days of Lord Beaconsfield have hardly
died away.

The ostensible causes of war have, indeed, recently
most frequently been connected with frontiers.
Wars formerly were often—in fact, during the
eighteenth century were chiefly—the outcome of
dynastic ambitions or intrigues. The wars of
religion have been strenuous and terrible. The
ambition and oppression of a single man has more
than once plunged a whole continent in blood.
Peoples, struggling for their freedom, have appealed
to the sword, and fought long and fiercely for their
lives. But the most important wars during the last
century have been those erroneously ascribed, for the
want of a better term, to frontier disputes. The
Franco-German War, it has often been said, was
for a frontier; the title of one of the many works
dealing with it was "The War for the Rhine
Frontier." The war of 1864 was waged by
Germany to recover the duchies of Schleswig
and Holstein on her frontier with Denmark. It
led to the war of 1866, and the war of 1866 led to
that of 1870. We have twice fought Afghanistan
about frontier incidents. Frontier questions in
Asia have placed us on the brink of war with
Russia more than twice. We have seen Japan at
grips with Russia about a frontier State—Korea.
We almost came into collision with France over a
very distant frontier incident at Fashoda.

The most interesting study, therefore, of soldiers
who look beyond tactical and minor strategical
questions is connected with the frontier line, where
we impinge upon territory potentially hostile. The

most urgent work of Chancelleries abroad and of our Foreign Office is connected with the creation of conventions as regards frontiers and the removal of sources of discord at places where our territories adjoin those of other nations.

Some people look for the day when the world will all be accurately mapped out and divided, and the beneficent sway of international law will keep all nations within their boundaries, all patient and unaggressive, all contented and all appeased. But law without force behind it constitutes as impotent a threat as a leadless pistol or a spiked gun. Before the tribunal of nations, unless all nations coalesce in a manner other than is usual with them, might will still have its own way, whether sanctioned by international law or not. Moreover, to imagine that if frontiers are exactly delimited war will cease, is to confuse the real and ostensible cause of former quarrels between nations. What really brought about the greater struggles we have named was not a sentimental question of frontiers, but a far more impelling force—namely, that due to race expansion. It was this mighty power, with perhaps religious enthusiasm behind it, which forced a nation out of boundaries too small to hold it, and caused it to surge over the landmarks of its neighbours. It is a force of Nature, such as that which drives the rising tide, that at certain epochs in its history urges a nation onward ; an impulse very different from the desire for a clearly marked and defined boundary such as a river or the apex of a mountain range.

The Franco-German War of 1870 was, no doubt,

in a limited sense a war for a frontier, and was the outcome of that of 1866 ; but it was the ambition of Prussia to take up a leading place amongst the States of Germany, and to seize the commanding position to which she felt she had risen, that brought about the " seven weeks " war. When France and Germany, as a result of 1866, were brought in contact, it was the same vigorous growth of a virile people, with the advantage of a commanding genius to advise and lead them, that brought about a struggle that was inevitable.

Similarly, it was not the necessity for a Rhine frontier that urged great French warriors from Francis I. to Napoleon III. to make it their ambition to gain the line of that river ; but it was the prolific ambition and expansion of force of the French race, to which their rulers gave expression, that made a frontier a pretext for war. Again, Japan and Russia came into collision in the Far East because Japan needs room in Korea for her expansion, and Russia needs similar expansion towards the sea for her land-locked inhabitants.

But if we cannot entirely avert war by setting up conventions and ensuring accurate cartography, we can at least minimize the chances of its outbreak by removing stumbling-blocks and misinterpretations, and by securing well-informed discussion before an ultimatum is despatched. A knowledge of geography is of advantage to others as well as to soldiers, and, indeed, the latter would ofttimes be more fairly criticized were such knowledge more prevalent.

In this connection, attention may well be directed

to the frontier of Natal as it existed before the South African War. While that war was still imminent I remember that some of our greatest statesmen and many of our most confident advisers in the Press told us to hold Lang's Nek. They drew their conclusions from the map. Flowing to the southeast of that pass there was to be seen the Buffalo

SKETCH-MAP OF NORTHERN FRONTIER OF NATAL.

River, duly coloured blue. To the west the range of the Drakensberg appeared to forbid incursions from the Orange Free State. At certain seasons of the year the Buffalo is a formidable barrier; at others it is as dry as Piccadilly on a summer's day. Many of us have walked across it without wetting our feet. Therefore it offered no obstruction to the passage of the Boers. The Drakensberg is a rugged mountain range, but it is intersected by

many passes other than those shown upon the map.
Wherever a man can set his foot, we have the
authority of Napoleon and of Frederick for
asserting that an army may move. The Drakensberg was therefore no greater obstacle than the
Buffalo. The line of communications of a force
at Lang's Nek might be cut from either east or
west. A stronghold there could be isolated, and
could exert no strategical influence on the campaign
unless its garrison were of such abnormal propor-
tions and resources as to possess the power and
radius of action of a field army. Again, why, it
was sometimes asked, did not the column marching
to the relief of Ladysmith move away from the
railway and advance on that town from the east ?
On paper such a move was no doubt possible ; in
practice the absence of good roads and water
rendered it so difficult and so hazardous that the
route along the railway, in spite of its strategical
and tactical disadvantages, was preferred.

Here are a few instances that will stir us
all, where interest in, and familiarity with, the
geographical conditions of a comparatively small
district will make my remarks appeal specially to
British officers. We may remember, too, that a
British general has often been asked to suddenly
assume the rôle of diplomatist, and has been called
from the field of battle to trace a new frontier line
upon a map. A man liable to be placed in a position so responsible must be imbued with a sense of
strategical geography from his youth. The lessons
which stay with us we learn young. It is too
late to try your 'prentice hand in middle age

at conferences where issues are determined that may remain potent for good or ill through generations.

A few years ago people were suddenly aroused by certain disturbing incidents in the Sinaitic Peninsula, and the advantages or disadvantages of deserts as frontiers were much discussed. We shall in all probability hear more on the same topic in the near future, for, as will later on be shown, railway construction is the antidote to deserts, and Asia Minor has lately seen an unusual exhibition of energy in that direction. While deserts as frontiers must, of course, always influence military operations, where obstruction or passive defence alone are in view, they offer the greatest advantages of any.[1] Sir Charles Dilke and Mr. Spencer Wilkinson years ago, in their book on *Imperial Defence*, pointed out how a Russian army, moving on India viâ Penjdeh, Herat, and Kandahar, would, even should it arrive at Sakkur, still be far from, the centres of Indian life. A desert, it is true, with its terrors half annulled by the spread of civilization but still an inhospitable region, would then lie between the invader and regions where an inroad would be seriously felt, and where supplies for his consumption could be found. The Kalahari desert, again, is a protection to the Transvaal from incursions from Damaraland or Namaqualand. Railways have lessened the difficulties of the Sinai Peninsula since Napoleon studied them, but railways take a long time to push forward, and before an invasion of Egypt from the north can become an imminent danger, railways will have to

---

[1] Napoleon placed deserts, mountains, and rivers as obstacles on the frontiers of states in order of merit as stated.

be carried southwards to the two caravan routes
that traverse a region of which we have lately heard
so much. Of these routes, that on the west runs
by El Arish to El Kantara, on the eastern bank
of the Suez Canal ; the other from Kalaat-el-
Akabah, at the head of the Gulf of Akabah,

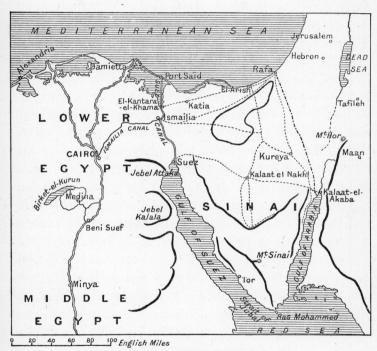

SKETCH-MAP OF THE SINAITIC PENINSULA.

through Kalaat-en-Nakhl to Suez. In either case
some 150 miles of desert have to be crossed,
and the problem of supplying water to his army
will trouble the invader. Food, forage, and fuel
cannot be obtained on the spot, and, in truth,
the factor of supply is so predominant that,
until secure bases, fed by railways have been estab-

lished at El Arish and Akabah, the operation
of invading Egypt by land from the regions on
the eastern shores of the Mediterranean will,
thanks to geographical conditions, scarcely come
within the category of normal operations.

The character of the coast which flanks these
routes is of importance to a Sea-Power such as we
are. On the Mediterranean, from El Arish to El
Kantara, it offers little or no facility for a landing,
save at Port Said and in the neighbourhood of the
former place. East of Port Said a long strip of
land encloses a lagoon, and it is not till within
20 miles west of El Arish that any menace from
the sea would threaten an army marching on Egypt.
On the southern route it is only the extremities,
again, which are open to a blow from the sea. At
Akabah small warships could closely approach the
shore, while at Suez the approach of ships is easy.

Deserts can, however, be created by diplomatic
action as well as by Nature. As long as international law is respected, a region can be denied
to certain countries, or may by international agreement be made forbidden ground for anyone but a
seeker of health or pleasure. Such neutralized
countries are termed " Buffer States," and play a
large part in diplomatic and military geography.
In order that warning may be given before the
actual soil of a nation is trodden by a powerful
invader, a " buffer State " is erected between them,
just as a potentate's reception-room is guarded by
antechambers, through which intruders are obliged
to pass ere they meet the great man. To us such
buffers are specially interesting, for we have availed

ourselves freely of this modern method of keeping trouble at arm's length.

Sometimes, however, regions or zones, neutralized by diplomatic conventions, are intended to conceal and prepare for projects of aggression rather than to provide against them. The Franco-Siamese Treaty of 1893, the neutral zone between Great Britain and Germany, created in the hinterland of the Gold Coast in 1888, furnish examples of these fictions, but there are several other instances of such subtleties that must sometimes puzzle the modern student of geography.

It is, however, enough for us here to consider the position of real buffer States—*i.e.*, of countries possessing national existences substantiated and guaranteed by treaties executed by great Powers with the object of preserving a *status quo*.

Switzerland, from her geographical situation, offers perhaps the best illustration of such a State, and of the strategical influence which attaches to it. She projects from the French frontier so as to make a salient between South Germany, Austria, and Italy. If France were to invade Southern Germany, she would find her movements flanked from the bend of the Rhine near Basle to Lake Constance, supposing the Swiss to be in alliance with Germany. In possession of Switzerland, on the other hand, France could threaten the flank and rear of a German force defending the line of the river from Basle northwards, as Moreau and Napoleon were not slow to recognize in 1800.

With the Swiss on the side of the French, a German army advancing by way of Breisach or

Strassburg would leave an enemy on the left flank of its communications. Or, again, with the Swiss against her, and Northern Italy the goal of France, and Milan or Venice or Verona the objective, the left of a French army would be threatened throughout.

Thus Switzerland, in point of numbers a very minor State, by its geographical situation exercises an enormous influence on European strategy. While her integrity is respected, her voice is still a powerful one in the council-chambers even of the greatest Powers, and we may be sure that every mile of her river valleys and mountain passes are carefully studied by the General Staffs of all the countries of the Continent.

We have heard much lately of her powers of defence. The fitful breeze of popular favour is blowing just now in her direction, whether with sound reason behind it is a matter of doubt. Switzerland is a home of freedom, and in this respect is associated with England — that spot sacred from invasion, and set by Providence in a silver sea, apart, and secure. We know that Milton long ago spoke of the voice of Freedom dwelling amongst the mountains of Switzerland as it dwelt in the seas that surround England. Popular imagination perhaps ascribes the continued independence and national security of Switzerland to the fact that it is a land defended by Nature against oppression, esconced in mountains that defy invasion, and inhabited by a population placed in security by a special Providence. Such, however, is not the case, and, in considering the relative securities of England

and Switzerland, we would do well to bear it in mind. Switzerland is so situated that it is in the interests of all her neighbours to preserve her territory intact, while she has no, nor ever can have, need to carry her armed forces across her own frontiers. It would suit none of the great Powers to sub-divide her territory between them. Her mountain passes constitute menaces and checks in different directions, and prevent the aggression of one great Power against another. Switzerland has no foreign possessions to be given as spoil to the victor. With us it is different. It would be to the interests of many great Powers could our possessions all the world over be subdivided amongst them. The dis-appearance of England would mean the partition of a great estate, the destruction of Switzerland merely the extinction of an individual.

She, in fact, like some other European kingdoms, owes her existence less to her military efficiency than to the rivalries of powerful neighbours.

Once the highway of the French armies under Napoleon, she was neutralized by eight Powers in 1815, when the great Emperor finally fell. Belgium, the cockpit of Europe, was neutralized by five Powers in 1831. Little Luxemburg pre-serves an existence between the upper and lower millstone because it was neutralized by five Powers in 1867. The existence of a State which hangs on neutralization is of course precarious. The power of the countries which guarantee the neutrality may ebb or flow, and the security varies with them. But a neutralized country, if not absolutely immune from violation, is far less open to aggression than it would otherwise be. The State which proposes to tear up the treaties that safeguard it usually faces a task of great magnitude, and will think twice before it proceeds to action.

To go farther afield, Abyssinia is not a buffer State, as are Switzerland and Afghanistan, but its integrity is guaranteed by Britain, France, and Italy, and it supplies an illustration of a diplomatic convention obstructing the processes of Nature, and preventing the creation of a frontier by unrestrained natural forces. The integrity and independence of Persia have only just lately been guaranteed by Russia and Great Britain, and in this case a real buffer State is created between the dominions of two great Powers threatening to impinge on one another. This latter case, however, furnishes us with a new departure in geographical delimitation, because, while spheres of interest for Russia and England are created on the north and east respectively, a zone offering opportunities to both Powers is left between them.

An example of a State which has drawn neutralizing pledges from two Powers without being between them occurs in the case of Tibet, which can scarcely be described as a buffer State between Great Britain and Russia, because, while she is contiguous with the possessions of one, she has no territorial contact with the other.

At both extremities of the line of the Indian Empire we have buffer States. The Durand Agreement signed at Kabul in 1893 drew a line between the tribes under British and those under Afghan influence, for the entire distance from

Chitral to Seistan, and the Indian Empire gained
a frontier which is accurately delimited. At one
end of the line we have protectorate buffers to our
frontier in Nepal, Sikkim, and Bhutan, while on the
north-eastern territory of Upper Burma we have a
fringe of protected States known as the Upper
Shan States. At the other end we find Afghanistan
and the buffer strip of Wakhan.

Moreover, in the case of our Indian Empire, so
much anxiety have we displayed to keep our frontiers
with Russia apart that the astonishing result is seen
in Great Britain having a three-fold frontier to the
North-West of India—namely, (*a*) the administrative border of British India to (*b*) the Durand line,
or frontier of active protection, and (*c*) the Afghan
border, which may be said to be our outer or
advanced strategical frontier.[1]

Lord Curzon in his Romanes Lecture has also
pointed out how diplomatic fictions and conventional
delimitations are carried further when two Powers,
although they create what may be termed a buffer
State, admit that the political influence of one
party to the agreement may predominate. Thus,
Korea is a buffer State between Japan and China,
but under the unchallenged influence of Japan.
Afghanistan, again, occupies a similar situation
between Great Britain and Russia.

Protectorates are another variant of the diplomatic
conventions which neutralize countries or create
buffer States. The Russian scheme of protectorates
includes Khiva and Bokhara, and aimed at Manchuria and Korea. Tunis is a French protectorate,

---

[1] Romanes Lecture, by Lord Curzon, 1907.

and Morocco may become one. Our policy in India has been one of protectorates. The partition of Africa proceeds by much the same method under another name. Where the protectorate shades away into a sphere of influence it is difficult to define. It would be necessary to consider the circumstances of each case separately ; to lay bare the forces which have been at work—political, commercial, or perhaps strategical, often a combination of all three. Sometimes we can trace the cause plainly enough. Somaliland lies under the shadow of our arm because we must safeguard the food-supply of Aden. There is such a thing, too, as a "sphere of interest." The degradation in point of importance appears, in fact, to be the protectorate, the sphere of influence, and the sphere of interest. The protectorate is quite definite. The sphere of influence means that the Power asserting the claim denies the right of any other exterior Power to assert itself in the territory so described, but the nature of the responsibilities assumed varies with each case, and must be widely different according as the country in question possesses an independent government, as does Persia, or is inhabited by semi-barbarous tribes, such as are found upon the Niger. While a sphere of influence is less clearly defined than a protectorate, it is more developed than a sphere of interest, which is often its embryo stage of existence.

The modern theory of "Hinterland" is another development of the doctrine of the sphere of influence, a theory more useful, perhaps, as a potential weapon for extension of territory than for the protection of that already held.

Another curious variant of protectorate and sphere of influence is that of tenant. Proud potentates assume an attitude of humility, and are prepared to become tenants of semi-barbarous peoples, in order to conceal a policy of encroachment and allay the resentment of rival Powers. We ourselves, the sovereigns of India, have become the tenants of humble neighbouring potentates, for we have acquired Quetta and Nushki on quit-rents in perpetuity from the Khan of Kelat. Germany has only a lease of Kiao-chao. Russia had only a lease of Port Arthur, and we, as occupants of Wei-hai-wei, are the tenants of China. Kow-loon on the mainland of Hong Kong, necessary to the security of that important naval base, is held nominally by lease, and is not, properly speaking, a British possession, although absolutely indispensable to the security of Hong Kong.

Finally we come to the most impalpable form of a sphere of influence yet devised—that by which a weaker State promises a more powerful one that she will not alienate any portion of her territory to any other Power. This is a variant of the principle of a first refusal in the case of a sale in civil life. It gives one Power a kind of reversionary claim to the estate of another, is the first step towards a sphere of influence, and may often lead, little by little, through protectorate, to absorption.

CHAPTER III

SOME EUROPEAN FRONTIERS

As has been said, few or no Continental countries possess what can be called natural frontiers, but their existing boundaries are the resultants of opposing forces. The ambition or energy of rulers, the forces of expansion inherent in virile races, geographical conditions, have all alike been modified, subdued, or twisted, by the forces of reaction they created, by combinations of nations, by diplomatic intervention. The frontiers of Europe are historical records, eloquent of the great human catastrophes that have moulded them, rather than witnesses to the progress of geological formations or, save in certain cases, the influence of geographical features. Since, however, military geography gathers within its purview the changes in the conditions of a country which man has brought about, a subject of vast interest is opened to the military student when he enters on an examination of how the various nations have dealt with the problems of frontier defence confronting them.

Every variety can be found, every anomaly from every rule, all, however, carefully thought out, weighed, and considered, all representing some principle of strategy established by the best brains of which each nation could avail itself. To deal with every frontier, explain every departure from the line marked out by Nature, and examine the reasons for variety of treatment, would demand time and space and leisure of which the writer cannot hope to avail himself. But enough may be said to give an indication of what remains behind, and of fields where others may perhaps penetrate when opportunity offers.

Our ally France has perhaps the most eventful history of our neighbours. Her frontiers have expanded and contracted, and like high-water marks on the beach have advanced or receded with the storm. The story of her frontiers is the military history of France.

In the following pages dealing with the French frontier, fortified places have been spoken of as belonging to three classes. The first class comprises those which, owing to their importance, should be always completely equipped both with *personnel* and *matériel*, provisions, and supplies of all kinds, and should be ready to undergo a siege of long duration. Those of the second class are maintained to lend support to active forces operating in their neighbourhood. Such are kept up as regards garrisons, armament, stores, and supplies, to certain standards, which are determined by the Government according as circumstances may dictate. The third class includes forts and works, which are neither armed, nor manned with special garrisons, nor provisioned, in peace-time, but are occupied and looked after by the military establishments which they contain, and are regarded as fortifications to be utilized in case of necessity.

The northern frontier of France extends from Dunkirk to Longwy, and is some 220 miles long. It constitutes the boundary between France and Belgium, and is of the greatest interest to us, therefore, because we are one of the Powers who

SKETCH MAP OF N.E. FRONTIER OF FRANCE.

have guaranteed the integrity of that kingdom, and it is this neutrality which is the strongest defence of this frontier.[1]

The principle underlying the scheme of defence has been the organization of a central defensive position between the Scarpe and the Sambre, which should menace hostile lines of advance

---

[1] By the Treaty of London, November 15, 1831, the neutrality of Belgium was guaranteed by Austria, Russia, Prussia, France, and Great Britain.

either to its east or west. It will be convenient
to discuss this frontier in five sections, taking the
first as extending from the sea to the River Lys.
Here we find the fortified towns Calais, Grave-
lines, Dunkirk, and Bergues. The geographical
features of the country, however, supply more
formidable obstacles, for all the neighbourhood to
the River Yser could be inundated with considerable ease, and is not, therefore, to be traversed by
hostile forces without immense difficulty. From
the Yser to the Lys the frontier is again secured
by potential inundations from that river and the
Neuf-Fossé Canal. *eastwards*

Continuing south-~~westwar~~ds, we find the second
section stretching from the Lys to the Scarpe. Lille,
thanks to its circle of detached forts (for its enceinte
is obsolete), is the main support of this line, and a
fortress of considerable importance, covering as it
does the junction of several lines of rail connecting
with the interior of France. Douai, the fort of
Scarpe, and the citadel of Arras, may be regarded
as obsolete.

It is in the next section, that between the Scarpe
and the Sambre, that the position already referred
to is found. Its right flank rests on Maubeuge
(a fortress of the second class), on the Sambre, and
the forest of Mormal, while its left would be covered
by the inundations of the Scarpe and Scheldt.
Here on the Scarpe and Scheldt we find the *forts
d'arrêts*, of the third class, Maulde, Flines, and
Courgies, intended to protect the sluices on the
river and the means of inundation which they
supply. The strong places, Condé, Landrecies,

Cambrai, Valenciennes, Bouchain, and Le Quesnoy, which were formerly formidable, are now more or less obsolete.

In the fourth and next section we come upon the Valley of the Oise, constituting the " Trouée de Chimay," through which the shortest road to Paris enters the frontier. The western end of this section of the line is protected by Maubeuge, and the other by the forests of Thiérache. But the Trouée de Chimay, in the centre of the line, leaves the gate of invasion wide open ; a *fort d'arrêt*, Hirson, has accordingly been constructed to block the path, which a French writer has termed an outpost rather to herald than hold back an intruding force. Former strongholds in this neighbourhood —Mézières on the Meuse, Givet, Guise on the Oise, and Rocroy—are now obsolete.

The fifth and last section we shall have to discuss extends to the point where French and German territories begin to march together, and is protected from the north by the line of the Meuse and by the fortress of Montmédy (second class). Longwy, at the end of the line, can no longer be included in the list of modern fortifications. A series of positions have been prepared as a second line to further add to the strength of those just referred to. These are the line of the Somme (on which are situated Péronne and Arras, fortifications no longer up to date), intended to meet any menace from the west on the central position between the Scarpe and the Sambre ; and the position Laon-La Fère, which, with its detached forts, Laon and La Fère (both of the third class), covers the district between the Aisne on the south and the Somme on the north.

The eastern frontier of France extends for some 240 miles from Longwy to Delle, lying westwards of the bend of the Rhine at Basle, and forms the

SKETCH MAP OF PART OF N.E. & EASTERN FRONTIER OF FRANCE.

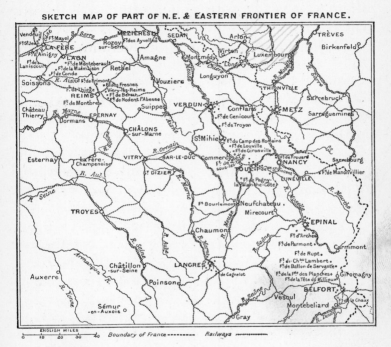

dividing line between Luxembourg, Germany, and France.

The line of defence runs almost straight south-eastwards from Mézières, through Verdun, Toul, and Épinal, to Belfort. Between Mézières and Verdun lies a region that offers a line of advance to Germany, open save for the obstacle furnished by the line of the Meuse. Verdun itself is a fortress of the first class, and is placed on the direct road from Metz to Paris. A ring of works constructed on both banks of the Meuse have converted it into an entrenched camp, capable of accommodating a powerful force. From Verdun the line is continued along the Meuse, defended by forts established on both banks of that river, known as Forts Genicourt (this fort has, however, now been included in the defences of Verdun), Troyon, Camp des Romains, Liouville, Gironville, Jouy-sous-les-Côtes, all of which are of the second class. Thus we reach Toul, likewise a fortress of the first class, and situated on the direct line of rail from Paris to Strassburg. Its defences include a great entrenched camp surrounded by forts, erected on both banks of the Moselle. The forest of Haye, which has been treated so as to furnish a considerable obstacle, lies just beyond the circle of defences on the east. The defence of this forest is supported on the left by the first-class fort Frouard, while on the right a fort of similar class—Pont-Saint-Vincent—fulfils a similar duty. A fort, Pagny-la-Blanche-Côte, of the third class, has been further provided to prevent the defences of Toul being turned from the south.

Between Toul and Épinal exists a second *trouée*, through which a line of operations of an invading German might naturally extend. This opening is covered only by the line of the Moselle.

In front of the defences of Toul a fort of the first class has been constructed at Manonviller, eight or nine miles east of Luneville, in order to protect the line of rail leading east from Nancy ; and behind it, to the south-west, near Neufchâteau, the fort Bourlemont, of the second class, protects an important railway junction. Proceeding southwards we reach Épinal, another fortress of the first class, comprising a third great entrenched camp protected on both banks of the Moselle by a circle of forts as in the cases of the other two. From Épinal the line of defence follows the high ground on the left bank of the Moselle, and is strengthened by the forts D'Arches (which, however, is now included in the defences of Épinal), Parmont, Rupt, Château Lambert, Ballon de Servance, which block the passages of communication between the valleys of the Moselle and the Saône. A day's march farther south, past the fort of Giromagny, included in them, now brings us to the defences of Belfort; and there again we find a first-class fortress, and an entrenched camp, protected by a circle of forts, with Fort de Chaux, lying somewhat beyond the perimeter on the southern side.

The fort of Mont-Bard and the defences of Lomont, farther to the south, are intended to command the avenues of approach which an enemy might endeavour to utilize in an attempt to turn the Belfort defences from the south.

As regards a second line: Behind the gaps between Mézières and Verdun, Toul and Épinal, are to be found the position of Rheims, and the fortress of Langres with its circle of detached forts. The former position, naturally strong, has been reinforced by certain detached works of the third class. Langres and its defences are only to be placed in the third class, except Fort Cognelot, in the neighbourhood, which guards an important railway and belongs to the first class. In the event of an invader violating the neutrality of Switzerland, and making an attempt to turn Belfort and its defences from the south, he would be met by the fortress of Besançon, a fortress of the second class which also forms a support to the line of defence of the frontier on the Jura side. Dijon, a third-class fortress, similarly covers the south of Langres, and is intended to dominate the defile by which the Burgundy Canal and the line of rail enter the mountains of the Côte d'Or.

Behind the whole of these fortresses and works lies Paris, regarded as the central *réduit* or keep of the country, strengthened by all imaginable means, and garnished with a system of works whose perimeter measures about eighty miles.

In considering the French frontier in relation to the defence of the country, what strikes one in the first place is the arbitrary position that the line of demarcation everywhere assumes. That on the north was traced in 1815 to set limits to the ambition of France, the bugbear of the day, and prevent her pushing forward in that direction. The line was, in fact, intended to give advantages to the newly created kingdom of the Netherlands, should an invasion of France become necessary, rather than to provide the latter with a strong frontier. Neither had Nature any hand in tracing the line of 1871, which again recorded the humilia-tion of France, and placed her at strategical dis-advantages as compared with the period before the war.

Secondly, we must notice the two curious openings left in the long line of *forts d' arrêts*, deliberately inviting an entrance in the case of the northern one, in order that the intruder may be crushed by the troops massed in the great entrenched camps on either side.   The more southern opening, it is said, represents a sally-port through which the advance of the French troops may be directed against their traditional enemy.   This intricate system of forts and entrenched camps may again render possible a great concentration of troops in the south, which would march from thence northwards to strike the flank of the invader pressing on towards Paris. What renders this policy of entrenched camps and fortresses interesting from the geographical point of view, is that it illustrates the efforts of an especially scientific nation to neutralize the geographical weakness which her misfortunes have imposed upon her, and to obtain security by calling in the aid of artificial obstacles.   That the policy was based on a minute investigation both of the physical geography and topography of ground we may be very sure, and, good or bad, it represents the untiring industry and deliberate intention of highly trained officers.

The actual frontier line did not lend itself to defence—it was necessary to fall back to find the requisite positions ; but, as Marga has pointed out, it was most undesirable to relinquish to the enemy more French soil than was absolutely necessary, and thus a difficult problem was created which has demanded exceptional treatment for its solution. It is not possible here to stray beyond the borders

of geography into the realm of strategy. We shall
not, therefore, discuss how far the solution arrived
at is sound or not. But is not passive defence
abhorrent to strategy? and the strategical counter-
stroke—is it not the weapon of the numerically
weak? Is France likely to be numerically stronger
than Germany? In attempting to cover everything,
we end in covering nothing, as the great Frederick
taught us in his "Instructions," while Napoleon,
in his *Correspondance*, has written: "On ne peut
défendre une frontière par un cordon sans être
faible partout, car tout ce qui est humain est
limité." On the other hand, French writers tell
us that the French forts are intended to act as
"centres of action" for field armies ready to give
one another mutual support. We cannot revive
again a controversy that was once brisk, but it is
allowable to point to the vast numbers of French
soldiers who must be locked up in these *points
d'appui*, or "centres of action," or whatever term
may be adopted to temporarily disguise their true
nature. One authority has placed that number
as high as 600,000 men. Possibly the estimate
is exaggerated, and the troops will be of the second
line, unfit for field service at the outbreak of war,
but the mere suggestion of such figures is disquieting. Nor is it reassuring to hear that there are
those in France who do not hesitate to condemn
the siting and construction of the works themselves.

But, to leave a thorny question, let us turn
our glance towards the Rhine, and note in what
a vastly different spirit her frontier problem has

been dealt with by Germany. She now possesses a natural boundary on part of her frontier, a geographical obstacle which was once in French hands—namely, the line of the Vosges Mountains. We do not find passes and lines of advance studded with numerous forts ; in fact, we discover no fortifications except the great entrenched camps of Metz and Strassburg, improved and stronger than before, on the flanks of this part of the line and intended to cover the concentration of great armies and the rail-heads from which some day, perhaps, they will be supplied and fed. The principle underlying this system is frankly offensive, and as in 1870 her troops poured into France by six main lines of rail, and enabled her to complete her strategical deployment before her rival's forces were fully mobilized, so will it be in future. Facilities for movement, more especially so by rail, are carefully studied and fostered. The great stations stand ready equipped with platforms and sidings where necessary, supplying accommodation ready for the disentrainment of vast numbers of men, horses, guns, and vehicles. Her carriages are constructed, however, so that disentrainment may be accomplished without these accessories. Her railways are, in fact, built for war as well as for commerce.

Behind the two great entrenched camps on the frontier flows the Rhine, with passages across it prepared so that their security shall be insured, and on each bank of the river a line of railway to afford lateral communication along the front. In the second line a few great strongholds taking the form of huge entrenched camps, where men and guns may be collected in security, sited at points of strategic advantage, usually on the banks of, and often at the junction of, rivers. Mainz, Coblenz, and Cologne, with the works in their neighbourhood, are examples of such entrenched camps. Neu Breisach, Diedenhofen, Bitsch, and Rastatt, on the other hand, represent the fortress type. Germany, it is evident, intends once more to take the initiative, and her treatment of the defence of her western frontier tells us as much, more especially so if the "dislocation map" of her system of quartering troops in peace-time (published by Müller-Sagan) be studied.

But the German Empire has other frontiers besides that separating her from France, which has always been of the highest interest to us. She has, in fact, a total frontier length of 4,570 miles, made up as follows : The North Sea shuts her in on the north for about 290 miles ; Denmark touches her along nearly 50 miles ; and farther east the shores of the Baltic are German for close upon 930 miles. As against Austria, she has a line of frontier, including Lake Constance, of some 1,400 miles ; while she marches with Switzerland for some 250 miles more. On the east, German and Russian soil are contiguous for 840 miles. The frontiers of France (240 miles), Luxembourg (110 miles), Belgium (70 miles), and Holland (some 380 miles), make up the rest of the huge total. Omitting the five frontiers that have been named first, which have a geographical basis, we see that, with the exception of the Vosges, these boundaries are purely arbitrary and conventional. Next to that with France, the frontier of Germany with Russia is most interesting, and we will turn for a moment from the Vosges and Rhine to the dreary stretches of sand and alluvial plains that once formed the cherished possessions of the Polish Kingdom. This boundary is most incongruous and presents a puzzling problem, while both Germany and Russia seem to derive advantages and disadvantages from its erratic trace. When we first glance at a map of the region, it would appear that a Russian army might in three or four days' time be at Breslau. The distance is quite short, and might be disposed of in a few marches. Further examination, however, shows that the frontier line of Germany on the north-east is threatening to Russia, whose natural frontier on the west should be the line of the Vistula. What is also remarkable is that this stream, the most striking feature of the country, is held, in defiance of geography, at various portions of its length, not only by Russia and Germany, but by Austria too. Germany, or rather Prussia, is, in fact, astride on both the Vistula and the Niemen, and thus she can check any advance of Russia towards Breslau and Berlin by threatening the right flank and rear of her advanced line of operations.

Berlin, unlike Paris, is an open town, and appears at first sight—if geographical distances were alone considered—precariously near the Russian frontier. Germany has, however, called in the aid of fortification in this region, and the distance, measured by time, which lies between her capital and the hostile frontier is immense. To the north, where the great river we have just named prepares to join the Baltic, an entrenched camp is prepared at Danzig, where likewise a coast fortress exists. Farther to the south we find a fortress of the first class at Thorn, and the passages of the Vistula (*Weichselübergänge*) in between are guarded by bridge-heads, the two points where the railways cross being covered by the fortresses of Gaudenz and Dirschau. Thorn and Danzig, like Metz and Strassburg, are in fact bastions commanding, as it were, the curtain between them.

The strong fortress of Königsberg at the mouth of the Pregel, with its entrenched camp, Pillau, and Memel on the coast, block the northern end of the long arm that Germany stretches to the north-east beyond the Vistula, where geographical conditions favour rapid movement, and where were fought the battles of Eylau, Heilsberg, and Friedland. But further to the south lies an inhospitable district of mud and sand, swamps and lakes. In winter frost might render such a country less impenetrable than in summer, but the absence of cultivation and of large supplies would render subsistence so difficult that it is doubtful whether a modern army would attempt to enter it. The single fortress of Boyen, near Lötzen, on the railway from Königsberg to Brest-Litovski in Russia, is therefore held sufficient to block the passage of an army which, operating from the south, might endeavour to cut off East Prussia from the remainder of the German Empire. An efficient railway system into East Prussia has also been developed, and the concentration of her armies and these railways will be covered by the features geographical and topographical just described.

The German frontier on the western boundary of Poland is secured through its geographical conditions, for marshes cover it for miles and miles. Where natural obstacles, such as these, do not stand in the way, strong fortresses bar the advance of an invader from the east. West of Thorn, Bromberg protects the railway bridges across the Netze; southward from that river stretch the marshes of Netze till the Valley of the Warthe is reached. Along this watercourse the path of the invader would be easy, and accordingly it is blocked by the entrenched camp established at Posen.

The basin of the Oder offers another line of advance leading to the neighbourhood of Berlin. Nature has furnished no obstacles here to check an inroad, and therefore the German General Staff have constructed the defences of Glogau to block the way of an invader. Still farther south the entrenched camp of Neisse, on the river of that name, and the fortress of Glogau, close another avenue of approach.

But Germany does not rely on her great fortresses alone. She possesses a network of railways running towards her Russo-Polish frontier, and has in her hands, therefore, excellent facilities for carrying troops eastwards to meet an enemy. On the other hand, only two great lines of Russian railways lead across the German frontier. The most northerly directly threatens Berlin, but the lines of rail pass through the great fortress of Thorn, and before they can be utilized that stronghold must fall. The other runs south-west to the extremity of the frontier with Germany, and would be of little value for a sudden inroad on that country.

Germany derives a further advantage from the railway systems which traverse the regions we are discussing, in that, though built with strategical ends in view, something also was allowed for commercial interests. Her railways have been beneficent, and along them have sprung up busy towns and villages and a population which is making the most of the resources of the country. The Russian lines were built at the nod of the autocrat, absorbed when he came to a decision in warlike considerations, and in them alone. Russia, in consequence, will not have private enterprise behind her as will her potential foe. The steel lines have penetrated the country, and are there, but comparatively little human progress has marked their path, and the State, except in a military sense, has profited but little from them. Viewed from another aspect, however, the small facilities for movement, and the unreclaimed wastes, appear as advantages rather than the reverse to Russia. She relies still, as she always has done, on the blank spaces on her map. The Niemen, the Bober, the Vistula, the Narew, the Drevenz, the Prosna, and the higher portions of the Warthe, with their marshy banks, all constitute obstacles not to be despised. Behind them, too, lies a Russian Quadrilateral. The great fortress of Novo Georgievsk, with eight detached forts, covers the confluence of the Narew, the Vistula, and the Bug.

A little further south, on the Vistula, we find Warsaw, the capital of Poland, with a girdle of eighteen detached forts round her, Ivangorod, where the Wieprz joins the Vistula, and Brest-Litovski, a vast supply depot with another girdle of forts, on the Bug. This important strategical point guards the sole line of rail which crosses the miles of marsh that border muddy Poland, and here the various communications from the north and south meet the line of rail that leads eastwards into the heart of the Empire of the Czars.

In the second line stands Geography. The dreary wastes, the lone distances, the pathless solitudes that still are the features of the region—though several minor fortresses, and forts semi-obsolete and feeble, are also to be found—remain, as ever, the true defences and the bulwarks of the State.

Of the frontiers of Austria-Hungary, that which has for us the greatest interest is the north-eastern. Jutting out between Russian Poland and Roumania, Hungarian territory flanks the avenues of approach of a Russian force moving from Bessarabia through Roumania or Servia on Budapest. An advance through Bulgaria over the Danube towards Constantinople is menaced in like fashion.

The geographical position of the dual monarchy gives her a great strategical advantage, just as, to compare a smaller with a greater matter, the possession of the Dobrudscha by Turkey in 1877, projecting northwards and flanking the Russian left in their march across the Danube, exercised considerable strategical influence on the campaign of that year. Austria's strategical position, relative to an advance by Russia on Constantinople, is, in fact, decisive. Examined in greater detail, her frontier with Russia offers many curious anomalies and problems. Galicia is pushed beyond the great obstacle offered by the Carpathians, and the frontier is formed, in part at least, by the Vistula. It again crosses the San, where a natural boundary seems to offer, cuts the courses of the Bug, the Styr, the Dniester, and of several other rivers ; and is defined quite arbitrarily till it doubles back by the Transylvanian Alps to the Danube. Austria, obliged to resort to heavy fortification in Lombardy and Venetia, did not strengthen her Galician frontier till her relations with Russia were strained in 1854 ; then, no longer able to trust to friendly relations with her neighbour remaining undisturbed, she commenced to secure her north-eastern province. A great fortress and entrenched camp were constructed at Cracow. Powerful works at Przemysl and Lemberg have been added since. The passes of the Carpathians have been strengthened. Her railways have been developed with strategical objects in view ; she has, in fact, studied geography in relation to her diplomatic and strategical situations, and has altered the topography of her country in accordance with them.

She can also act offensively, in combination with her ally Germany, by operating against the left flank of any Russian army advancing westwards into the territory of her neighbour. Sir Frederick Maurice has told us that, in all probability, she will not fall back to the line of the Carpathians if attacked by Russia in Galicia, but will more

probably hold the lines of the rivers San, Wys-
loka, and Donajec successively, and threaten the
flank of a Russian force which might attempt to
ignore the force in Galicia and cross the Carpathians by the traditional line of ancient invasion
from Kiev on Budapest. The route known as the
" Magyar's Road " traverses one of the easiest de-
pressions of those mountains, and can be supplemented by several other passes in the neighbourhood.

The geographical characteristics of Italy and of
her frontiers possess anomalies which make them
interesting. At first sight Italy appears to be so
situated as though intended to become the cradle
of an independent and powerful nation. Separated
from the remainder of Europe by the masses of the
Alps on the north, the sea, which girdles in the
remainder of the country and joins the feet of
the mountains, makes her almost an island. Either
mountaineers or seamen, the hardiest of mankind,
should apparently protect every spot on her borders.
Actually she has no natural frontier except the sea,
and even the waves do not shut her in as effectually
as they might. It is only on the west of her land
frontier that the mountains are so steep as to allow
her general boundary to run along their water-
partings, or, in the case of the Maritime Alps, along
the heads of the valleys on the French slopes.

But in the north the higher watercourses, forming
ultimately the tributaries of the Po and of the
rivers flowing to the Adriatic, do not belong to her,
and the Swiss Canton of Tessin and the Austrian
Tyrol are unhappily pushed forward into Lombardy.

On the north-east, again, the great mountains do

not help her, for Austria-Hungary has remained in possession of their passes, and commands the issues from them to the plains.   On the whole, therefore, Italy's land frontiers are weak.   The Alps have, moreover, never proved a formidable obstacle, and the attack, more especially so when a very indented frontier such as Italy's is in question, has usually got the better of the defence.   " The battles lost or won at the foot of the alpine passes and in the vine-yards of the great northern plain,"[1] have in ancient and modern times, from Rivoli to Bedriacum, decided the fate of Tuscany and Rome.

Moreover, her geographical formation, far too ex-tended for her breadth, has rendered communication between her various component parts very difficult, although steamships have come to the assistance of roads and railways, and have considerably improved matters.   Again, the plains of Northern Italy are perhaps the most fertile in Europe, while down the peninsula the country is usually mountainous, and, except for patches of fertility, is for the most part of little value.   The capital, finally, is badly placed. Too near the sea, and menaced, therefore, by expeditionary forces, it is widely distant from the centres of activity and from the important strate-gical points of the northern regions, and is not in secure communication with them.   The magic of her name and her immemorial traditions give a dignity to Rome which is unsurpassed amongst cities, but she is, nevertheless, an unsatisfactory capital for a united Italy.   The interior geographical features of the long peninsula are likewise unfavour-

[1] *Garibaldi's Defence of the Roman Empire,* by Trevelyan.

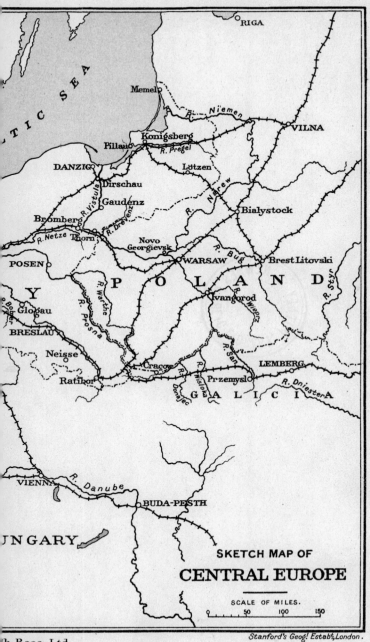

SKETCH MAP OF
CENTRAL EUROPE

SCALE OF MILES.

0   50   100   150

Stanford's Geog.ℓ Estab.ᵗ, London.

h Rees, Ltd.

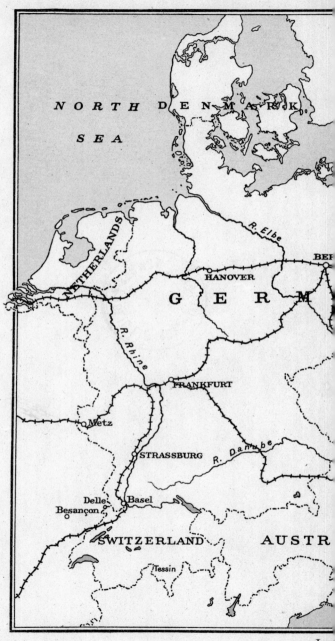

able to the defence of Italy. The long range of
the Apennines divides one side of her sea-frontier
from the other, and shuts them off from one
another ; while along the level strips of her coast-
line lateral communication may easily be interrupted from the sea. With her coast-line, enormous
relatively to her area, she should have become a
great Sea-Power, and will need still to become so,
if the problem of the defence of her frontiers is to
be satisfactorily solved. Though somewhat tardily,
the Italian navy has consequently received the
careful attention of her Government, and has been
fostered with a full sense of the importance that
attaches to its efficiency. Thus, geographical
peculiarities have exerted an immense influence on
the military policy of the youngest of the greater
European Powers, and the close association between
geography and strategy receive most complete
recognition in the case of Italian politics. It is
impossible to find a more striking illustration of
their close interdependence than in her case, and
the eternal influence of strategic features is
vindicated in her history from the Republic to the
present day. In the future they will very probably
influence her foreign politics in an ever-increasing
degree, and Italy may find it to her interests to rest
more and more on the naval strength an alliance
with a great Sea-Power may offer her.

The question of sea-boards and islands lying off
them brings us to consider some geographical conditions at the opposite end of Europe which have
lately attracted attention.

THE BALTIC AND ALAND ISLANDS

Within the last few months rumours that Russia proposed to fortify the Aland Islands have created considerable uneasiness, and those intent on watching South-Eastern Europe found their attention suddenly called to the Baltic. By the terms of the Treaty of Paris, concluded, as we all know, at the conclusion of the Crimean War in 1856, the Czar was bound "not to fortify the Islands or to maintain or create there a military or naval establishment." Less than fifty miles from the coast of Sweden, and less than a hundred miles from Stockholm, the Aland Islands lie in the centre of the entrance to the Gulf of Bothnia, and there such a naval base might be established as would be a standing menace to Sweden. The idea of strengthening a position of such considerable strategical importance in defiance of an existing agreement accounted quite sufficiently for the stir. But there was more behind. It was not the possibility that a potential *point d'appui* might be thus created that was obnoxious. No such strong measure as the denunciation of a treaty still in force could have been taken without Germany and Russia having entered into an understanding upon the question, and an understanding between these two Powers as regards the Baltic might have meant a very great deal indeed.

Was an attempt to constitute the Baltic a *mare clausum* going to be made by these two Powers? Would not such a claim create unrest in Europe such as might develop into war? Denmark and

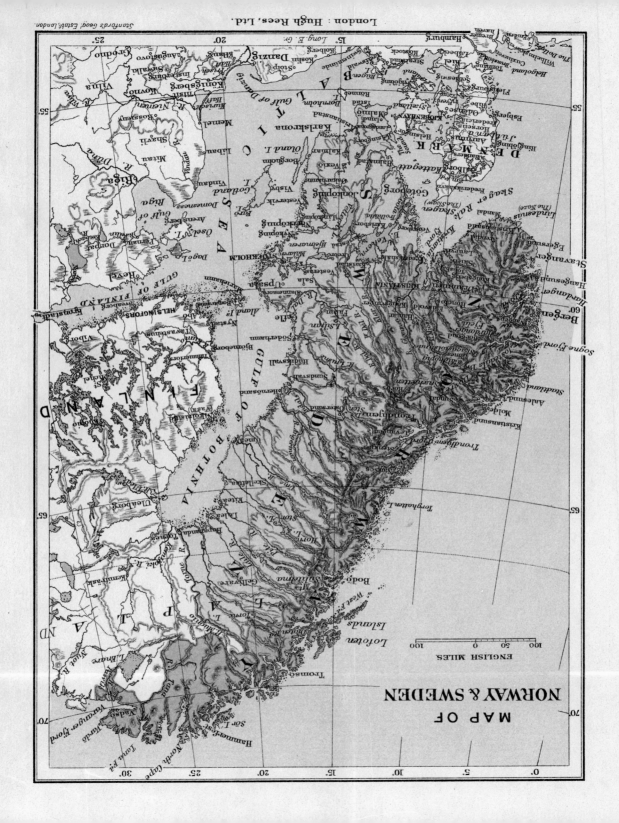

MAP OF
NORWAY & SWEDEN

ENGLISH MILES
100   50   0   100

London : Hugh Rees, Ltd.

Stanford's Geog¹ Estab⁺ London

Sweden would be very much affected by such a policy, but neither could greatly influence the actions of either of her mighty neighbours. As regards ourselves, small wonder if there were apprehension at the rumours! England as the greatest naval Power is obviously supremely interested in the freedom of all the seas, and in the independence of the weaker Baltic States. Could the Baltic be closed to a Power whose naval strength may try and force a powerful fleet through an entrance in Danish waters some fifteen miles in width? The discussion of questions such as these in the daily press was a cause for alarm in itself, and suddenly the Aland Islands and the Baltic question became, therefore, of an interest and importance for which their geographical situation could alone account. But since April, 1908, the sky has cleared; we can regard the Aland Islands and their strategical value for the present as examples of how geographical situations influence policy, and we can do so as a matter of academic interest. At the close of April an international agreement was signed in St. Petersburg, by which the four Baltic littoral Powers—that is to say, Russia, Germany, Denmark, and Sweden—agree to recognize the territorial *status quo* in that sea. Simultaneously a similar agreement with regard to the North Sea was signed by Great Britain, France, Germany, Denmark, Sweden, and Holland. The Treaty of Stockholm of 1855, by which Great Britain, France, and Sweden had entered into an alliance, was at the same time denounced by the three Powers concerned. It is to be gathered, therefore, that the safety of Sweden is secured by the agreement that has first been mentioned, and that the Aland Islands are not to be converted into a menacing naval base commanding the entrances to the Gulfs of Bothnia and Finland.

This leads us to consider the geographical position of Denmark. On the one side she abuts on the North Sea; on the other her shores are lapped by the Baltic. Thus, Denmark is intimately concerned in the strategical situation in both these seas, and both the recent agreements concerning them closely affect her. She could not consent that the *status quo* should be maintained on one side, and that she might be attacked on the other. We are furnished here with an illustration of strategical geography, and are taught to recognize how both North Sea and Baltic, geographically distinct, cannot be so treated when diplomacy and strategy make their influences felt.

The list of countries who have made themselves parties to this international engagement includes Holland; and, as a matter of course, the *status quo* on land of that country must be preserved if peace is to reign on the waters on which her ports are situated. It may be asked why Belgium has not been included in the conclave of Powers, and has received no guarantee of the preservation of the *status quo* in her territory when this latest addition to international engagements was made. The inviolability of Belgian soil is essential if peace is to be preserved in Europe; but the integrity of Belgium is guaranteed by treaties which have been respected for years, and are likely to continue to be respected.

CHAPTER IV

THE INFLUENCES OF GEOGRAPHICAL FEATURES ON OPERATIONS

MOUNTAINS

THE questions we have been discussing in connection with the Swiss and Austro-Hungarian frontiers suggest mountains and their influence on strategy to our consideration. They loom large in imagination and appear a formidable obstacle to an invader. The close student of war will, however, place less reliance on them. They are often, or even usually, regarded as specially favouring a defensive attitude ; but the Archduke Charles was very probably right when he contended that they offer greater facilities to the attack.

That they do especially favour the offensive-defensive rôle which is traditional in our Service is, however, undeniable. An intimate knowledge of mountain ranges, their valleys, their passes, and the communications through them will enable an active opponent to issue from them, strike his blow, and then retire again into fastnesses where it is difficult for troops without an intimate knowledge of the ground to follow. To compare small things with great, and furnish an illustration of what is meant, we may call to mind the forays of the Highlanders on the lowlands of Scotland ; the incursions of the hill tribes on our cantonments on the north-west frontier of India ; the attacks of the Boers descending from the mountainous regions of South Africa on our lines of communication during the late war.

But we are not here discussing forays or hill warfare such as are ever incidental to our army. We have greater events in view—the defence of a nation's frontier against a deliberate invasion, or the influences mountain ranges may exert on the progress of great campaigns.

It is not denied that a campaign amongst mountains offers immense difficulties to an attacking force. What is asserted is that an intimate knowledge of the ground will place advantages in favour of the general who possesses it such as will outweigh them. A range of mountains has to be watched for many miles ; but the proper way to defend it is not to try and strongly guard every pass ; to do so would infallibly lead to the condition of "strong everywhere, strong nowhere," which is the forerunner of disaster ; and a line of passes once pierced means something more disastrous than a position encroached upon. Lateral communication amid mountains is almost always so difficult that it is easier for the attack to reinforce and make good its foothold than for friends holding neighbouring passes either to send direct aid or relieve tension by assailing the flanks of the attack. On the other hand, it is right to point out that supply is a more difficult problem for the attack than the defence, and that geographical conditions may enable the defender to watch the crests of the ranges, concentrate his main force behind, and oblige the enemy as he issues from the hills to form front to a flank. Nevertheless, the balance of advantage will usually lie with the attack.

There are always several passes through or over every range of hills, and if pierced at any point the line of defence has to be abandoned. Marshal Saxe told us long ago that " however rough and impracticable mountains may at first sight appear, passes are nevertheless to be always found on being diligently sought for ; and even the knowledge of the inhabitants is often at fault because they use the passes they are accustomed to, and do not look for any others."

Popular tradition, in fact, and the inhabitants of a district are often most misleading guides, and it is essential that the features of the theatre of operations should be familiar at first hand to some officers of the staff of the general who wishes to make the most of its natural characteristics.

Graham's turning movement in 1813, through the inhospitable region drained by the headwaters of the Ebro, which the French then regarded as pathless mountains, furnishes us with an excellent illustration in this respect.

Where, however, the inhabitants of a mountainous region are united against the invader, much that has just been said should be modified. To conquer the whole population of a country is an almost hopeless task, as the Austrians found in Herzegovina and Bosnia, as we ourselves learnt during the late war in South Africa, and as Shamyl proved in the Caucasus between 1834 and 1859. His stubborn resistance, though few recognize it, has for us a special interest. For fifty years the inhabitants of the Caucasus defied the might of Russia—for themselves, their faith and country, as they saw it. But they fought too, unknowingly, for our security in India. "So long as the mountaineers resisted, they formed an effective barrier to the tide of onward conquest. When once they were swept away, there was no military or physical obstacle to the continuous march of Russia from the Araxes to the Indus." [1]

If the war be a national one for hearths and homes, the subjugation of mountainous districts is a tremendous undertaking. Discipline and armament, and even numbers, cannot assert their full influence. Cavalry are at a disadvantage, and fail to act as they should. Artillery cannot, except in the case of light mountain guns, be placed in position. A comparatively small number of active troops, turning their knowledge of the region to full account, may hold out for years.

But when the population is unable to combine for action, or is unwarlike, or is neutral, the situation becomes vastly altered, as the successful passage of many a forbidding mountain range by an army proves.

We have so often to fight amid mountains that the geographical features of mountains in relation

[1] *England and Russia in the East*, by Sir Henry Rawlinson, London, 1875, quoted in *The Russian Conquest of the Caucasus*, by John F. Baddely. Longmans, Green and Co., London, 1908.

to war should have a special fascination for us, and both from our own experience in invasions, such as in Abyssinia and the north-west frontier of India, and from the lessons of history which lie behind us, we should know how to appreciate their value as defences.

The Alps could not stop Hannibal; Francis I., too, crossed them in 1515 at the Col D'Agnello, some 10,000 feet above the sea, and subsequently fought the Battle of Marignano, or Melegnano, as the town from which it takes its name is now called. The so-called impassable Balkans have also been traversed by great armies more than once. We do not want to go beyond our own history to know that the Pyrenees are no insurmountable barrier. Napoleon, as we all remember, wiped the Alps away. In truth, if a mountain chain be an obstacle, it is also a screen, and behind it a commander may concentrate his forces unobserved, and may effect a passage by outwitting his opponent, just as has been done over and over again in the case of a broad river.

Alexander crossed the Hindu Kush from south to north in seventeen days. Two years later he passed from north to south in ten days. The Kabul Valley, the Swat and Buner districts, familiar to us, were all traversed by his men. Timurlane and Baba found no obstacle in these great mountains hundreds of years afterwards. The Suleiman range, too, has often been penetrated. From A.D. 1001 to 1027 Mahmud of Ghazni led his followers across it on no less than twelve occasions, moving by the Valley of Gomal and the Gwalari Pass to Dera Ismail Khan. The army of Jenghiz Khan crossed by the last-named pass at the beginning of the thirteenth century. The Kabul Valley and the Khyber Pass admitted Baba in 1527, and in 1740 Nadir Shah, striding from Kandahar to Ghazni and Kabul, reached the Indus by the same route. In 1839 and in 1878 our men trod in the footsteps of these old-world raiders ; and during the recent Tirah expedition we penetrated into the recesses of one of the most difficult countries in the world, and did so in spite of the disadvantages which a lack of geographical knowledge imposed upon us.

No passage of a mountain range by an army, however, excels in interest the astounding performance of a Chinese expedition which, in 1792, marched to the assistance of the Tibetans, whose country had been invaded by the Gurkhas. Over the towering mountains and snow-bound passes of Eastern Tibet a force of no less than 70,000 Chinese was led in two columns by General Sand Fo into the elevated regions of the plateau. The Gurkhas, defeated in two successive encounters, made their last stand on the river banks at Tadi, just above Nayakot, about 20 miles from Khatmandu. The Chinese wavered. Nor is it to be wondered at, when we remember that, before reaching Lhassa, their unwieldy force of 70,000 men had marched over 800 miles from their own frontier across one of the most difficult mountain routes in the world. Before meeting the enemy they had then advanced at least another 400 miles over uplands at elevations which were never less than 10,000 feet, involving the passage of many passes higher than Mont Blanc. They had suffered hardships, and were reduced in numbers. Their opponents were the best fighting men in Asia. To finish the story, it may be said that Sand Fo was a great general. He turned the leather guns which formed his field artillery on to the rear of his wavering troops, and drove them and the Gurkhas in front of them in one comprehensive sweep into the river. Then the Chinese trampled over friend and foe alike and speedily sacked Khatmandu. The barbarities inflicted on the conquered Gurkhas, ingenious and repulsive to an unheard-of degree, set seal to the victory. From that day to this, every fifth year, a deputation proceeds from Nepal through Lhassa to Pekin, and there offers tribute at the foot of the Chinese throne.

Such is the story of a punitive expedition which is perhaps unique. But what makes it especially remarkable and interesting to us is its connection with geography, and the accomplishment, by a race popularly regarded as incapable of producing an army, of a marching feat unparalleled in military history. The feat, which has also been referred to by Sir Clements Markham in his *Tibet*, is, in fact, a notable commentary, not only on the usual statements as to the inaccessibility of Tibet, but on prevalent criticisms applied to the Chinese soldier.[1]

But mountains may exercise an influence on the manœuvres of an army apart altogether from the question of their defensive application, and our own records from the Peninsula will supply us

[1] *Tibet the Mysterious*, p. 106 *et seq.*, by Sir Thomas Holdrich, K.C.M.G., K.C.I.E., C.B.   Alston Rivers, London, 1904.

with excellent examples of their effect on strategy.
Mountain ranges have hitherto been discussed as
direct obstacles and barriers to progress. They
have been viewed from the standpoint they offer
when they cut perpendicularly across a line of
operations. But obstacles may be very real in a
military sense, and yet run longitudinally rather
than perpendicularly to the line of advance. The
Monte Junto mountain ridge, between the Tagus
and the sea, perpendicular to the line of Wellington's
defence at Torres Vedras, limited Massena's attack
to one side of that chain, otherwise one wing of his
force might have been exposed to the concentrated
blow of his adversary.

The Sierra d'Estrella separates the Valley of the
Tagus from that of the Mondego, and the principal
roads leading from the Spanish frontier to the
capital of Portugal converge along the valley of
those rivers.

When Almeida fell it was uncertain by which
of the two valleys the French army under Massena
would endeavour to reach Lisbon. Both had to
be guarded, and the intervening range offered no
lateral communications between them. The Duke
of Wellington could not concentrate his force in
either valley without leaving the other open to his
opponent, and therefore that mountain chain was a
formidable factor in the strategical situation.

The influence of mountains on strategy is well
exemplified also in the military history of the war
of 1866, and the combinations of Moltke and the
perplexities of Benedek are standing examples of
how they may affect military operations.

Where, in fact, chains of hills or mountains split a country up, leaving long valleys between them, they enormously influence the movements of opposing forces. One can scarcely have a better example than the manner in which the mountains in the Shenandoah Valley biassed the strategy of "the valley campaign." The Massanuttons were a real asset to Jackson, who knew the ground, and had the intelligence to weave its natural features in with his design.

VALLEYS

It may be said that the first object of a general studying a country where hills exist should be to gain an intimate knowledge of the trend of its different valleys. He must ponder over the conformation of the region until his mind is, as it were, saturated with it. The little ruts and hillocks will gradually fade away, but a general impression, in which the great strategical framework stands boldly forth, will be left; the main water-sheds, that shape the valleys beneath them and link them one to another; the rivers, whose courses often mark the paths of access. In all ages of the past and in all of the future a mountainous district has been, and will be, held by occupying the valleys— that is to say, the communications through it.

Roads in the old days followed valleys, and now lines of rail have succeeded roads and often coincide with their course—the same reasons which governed the construction of a road governing that of a railway, though modern science has connected valleys together by tunnelling, and has enabled the railway to penetrate where roads could only climb with difficulty. The lines of valley, road, and rail are synonymous in geography; the paths of barbarian, Roman, and most modern general, follow the same groove. Old and new linked indissolubly together—one more illustration of the permanence of the principles of strategy and the enduring value of military history. The greatest commanders of recent times have not failed to commend to our notice the study of the campaigns of bygone ages and of generals long passed away. Nor need we be surprised when we reflect that the traveller of to-day, who starts from Constantinople for Vienna, follows a line of barbarian and Turkish invasion, by Adrianople, Philippopolis, Sofia, to Belgrade and Budapest, and is also on one of the great lines of communication of Imperial Rome. When we travel by Folkestone to Boulogne, and on to Chalons-sur-Saone and Lyons, we are again treading in the footprints of the legions.

VALUES OF STUDY OF HISTORICAL ROUTES

Alexander's career inspired the admiration of Hannibal [who placed him first of leaders], of Napoleon, and of Moltke, and we shall do well to study the campaigns of the great leaders that have astonished the world, and note how physical geography exerts its influence on strategy from century to century. The lines of communication which connected Alexander's army with its ultimate base in Greece will be utilized again some day; and once more, we may be sure, some leader of a great

enterprise will follow the Euphrates eastward, as
Alexander and Julian the Apostate did long years
ago. Indeed, seventy years back a modern strategist
was at work where the Macedonian had been before,
and where the Romans and Assyrians and Persians
had once marched and manœuvred. That was in
1837, when the Egyptians were trying to conquer
Asia Minor. Moltke, in the employment of the
Turks, reached the narrow defile through the Anti-
Taurus, which links Asia Minor to Syria, and the
strategical importance of the spot appealed to him
as hundreds of years before it had appealed to
Alexander. They say every great leader must have
a touch of imagination and poetry in his composition,
and certainly there are few more suggestive passages
than that which appears in one of Moltke's
letters[1] to his friend "F——," dated Diarbekir,
April 12, 1837. He describes the ravine below
the fortress of Zeugma, or Sigma, where the
Euphrates reaches its extreme western point, and
where in former days a bridge spanned it—perhaps
the reason why the Romans founded a colony in
so inaccessible a neighbourhood. He writes to his
friend : " One starlight night a little while ago I
stood on the ruins of the old Roman stronghold at
Zeugma. Deep below me, in a rocky defile, the
Euphrates glistened, the murmur of its waters
filling the stillness of the night. Then in the
moonlight passed before me Cyrus, Alexander,
Xenophon, and Julian. From this very spot they
too had once looked across the stream upon the

[1] Vide *Briefe über Zustände und Begebenheiten in der Turkei*, von
Helmuth von Moltke. Mittler und Sohn, Berlin, 1876.

realm of the Chosroes, and the prospect was the same then as now, for Nature here wears that stony aspect which changes not." Further, he goes on to tell how, as a libation to the shades of the departed, he flung a bottle of champagne his friend had given him into the abyss. When that passage is reached no doubt the confidence of the student sitting at the feet of a great master will be shaken. Did the high priest of closely calculated strategy and logical procedure really sacrifice at the shrine of mere sentiment ? Did the mathematically-minded Moltke lose his head ? A few lines more will reassure him, and the forethought of the strategist will be found vindicated in the words, " but I took the precaution to empty it first." He goes on to say that it was an excellent bottle, save for one fault. " It was the last."

RIVERS

It is not roads only, however, that follow the course of valleys. A great valley almost invariably implies a river. which is the geographical feature that perhaps most frequently affects strategical and tactical designs. Rivers have the same characteristics as military obstacles as have mountains, and are most usually treated as hindrances to advance not easily overcome. But their influence on strategy is far wider than this. They become strategical frontiers when their principal passages are strongly held. But their defence, like that of mountains, has hardly ever been successful for any length of time, and neither the Danube nor the Rhine has stopped the onward march of armies.

The Lower Danube, one of the greatest barriers in the world, has been crossed twenty times during a succession of Russo-Turkish wars, and that, too, in the face of defending armies. As a means of delay, however, they have in all ages proved of importance. The Po was of the greatest value in this way to the army of the Emperor Otho in A.D. 69,[1] as it has been, and will be, to more modern generals. Tactically they also constitute a natural line of defence in front of a position or on its flank. They may serve to safeguard the flank of an army while in movement. They may also dictate the direction of its march, because in certain countries they furnish water to troops where none is elsewhere obtainable, as when the flow of the Nile influenced Lord Wolseley, moving to the relief of Gordon, to follow the trend of the river. We may have a general knowledge of all the chief rivers of Europe, and of many of those in other parts of the world; but such superficial knowledge is inadequate for military purposes. In order to be able to calculate the advantages or otherwise rivers may afford to the movements of opposing armies, we must be familiar with their exact position in relation to the strategical points of the country; we must know the existing bridges and the nature of their construction, the ferries and fords, and the roads which lead to the points of passage. We must study the character of the river itself, whether it is rapid or sluggish, straight or winding; the nature of the bed, of the banks,

---

[1] *Civil War and Rebellion in the Roman Empire,* by Bernard Henderson, M.A. Macmillan and Co., London, 1908. Page 50.

and the relative altitude of those on either side. The Battle of the Yalu (April, 1904) and the incidents of the campaign of 1809, when the Lobau in the Danube sheltered the French from destruction, will serve to remind us that the presence of islands or otherwise must not be forgotten. Finally, as has been noted already, the effect of rain and the seasons of the year on the waterway should be accurately known.

If floods may render rivers impassable, intense frost may bridge them. In 1795, during the French invasion of Holland, French cavalry and horse artillery, moving over the ice, captured fourteen warships[1] wedged immovably in the frozen waters near Tesel. The horrors of the retreat from Moscow were piled up higher when the retreat was checked at the Beresina, where the ice-bridge, owing to the mildness of the season, had not formed.

RIVERS AS FRONTIERS

Rivers at first sight would appear the most natural frontiers for states, and indeed it seems as though Nature intended them for such, not only for reasons connected with military operations, but to facilitate civil administration.

A river defines a frontier so clearly that there can be no dispute regarding it. It is easy to note the persons who desire to pass it and the nature of the goods they may convey with them. To exercise control over them is the reverse of difficult. Yet it is a remarkable fact that there is not a single

---

[1] See Denison's *History of Cavalry*, p. 351, and for a fuller account, Appendix III.

state in Europe whose frontier is now marked by the course of a large river. The Rhine constitutes no frontier line ; no more does the Danube. Even little Switzerland, most compact of states, bulges out curiously into Baden across the Rhine at Schaffhausen. The land frontier of Portugal crosses at right angles the Douro, the Tagus, and the Guadiana. The Rhone, the Elbe, the Oder, the Vistula, the Po— not one of these mark the limitations of a state. Looking further afield, we find that the Indus is not the boundary of India, nor does the St. Lawrence delimit our possessions in Northern America.

It is true that the " Germany " of the Roman Empire signified the districts lying on the left bank of the River Rhine from Lake Constance to the sea. In those days there was the " Danube frontier," too. But such great rivers were then an efficient obstacle and line of demarcation between civilization and wild tribesmen, not between races possessed of organizations of relative equality.[1]

Frontiers have been discussed already, and no more need be said about rivers in that connection after attention has been drawn to this anomaly ; besides, we must pass on to examine another aspect of rivers which is worthy of particular attention.

RIVERS AS LINES OF OPERATION

When great streams flow parallel, or nearly so, to a line of operations, they form the most convenient highways for the transport of pro-

[1] *Civil War and Rebellion in the Roman Empire*, by Bernard Henderson, M.A. Macmillan and Co., London, 1908. Page 7.

visions and the warlike stores which are necessary to the existence of a modern army, and they may also be most useful when stores and supplies have to be accumulated at depots. The most ceaseless traffic does not impair the efficiency of a river route, which provides us with a channel not easily to be obstructed, and almost impossible to block. There is hardly a limit to the capacity of its transport, and for this reason a great river has often supplemented the efforts of sea-power and given it access to the interior, where its force would otherwise have been squandered in the shallows of a coast. Frederick the Great, during his various campaigns in Bohemia, utilized the carrying powers of the Elbe, and it formed his main line of communications. Supplies ascended the Pregel for Napoleon's invading force in 1812, and the Niemen was also utilized by him for the same purpose. In July, 1870, the leader of the second German army followed his example, and during the advance to the French frontier organized a flotilla of six steamers and a large number of tugboats to ply on the Rhine between Worms, Mayence, and Bingen as movable magazines. Purchases in Holland during the short period while its frontier was open loaded these vessels, which were filled also from the Lower Rhine and by such contributions as could be exacted from the stores available in the fortresses of Coblenz, Cologne, and Wesel. Later, when the Germans were marching rapidly into France, the great magazines in Bingen and Worms were replenished by the stores the river flotilla carried. When Burgoyne marched his force from Canada

down the Hudson towards Albany during the
operations which ended so disastrously for him
at Saratoga, the river parallel to the line of march
carried his baggage and stores and a month's
supply of food. Two hundred barges floated easily
along, while the troops laboriously forced their
way by roads half obliterated by the foresight of
their opponents. Every bridge they could have
made use of was destroyed, and their progress
was limited to a mile a day. But the great water-
way could not be interfered with, and the barges,
laden with a cargo " worth a king's ransom,"[1] were
gently carried onward by its flow.

Similarly, gunboats on the Nile facilitated and
assisted our advance on Cairo in 1801.

During the American War the Mississippi
enabled the ships of the Federals and the armed
forces they carried to penetrate into the inner-
most recesses of their opponents' country. Especially striking from the strategical aspect are
the operations conducted by Grant and Admiral
Foote up the Tennessee and Cumberland Rivers,
which are affluents to the Mississippi, in 1862.
The lines of communication of a Confederate force
invading Kentucky would be threatened by the
Federals moving up the Cumberland and Tennessee
Rivers from the Mississippi, with the control of
that great river in their hands. Western Tennessee
could not be occupied by the Confederates while
their opponents were masters of the river dividing
the State. A turning movement could be safely

[1] *The American Revolution*, by Sir George Otto Trevelyan, Bart.
Longmans, Green and Co., 1907. Part iii., p. 174.

made along that river which would otherwise be hazardous. Plans were accordingly made by which the ships of the North were called in to aid their armies, and the capture of Fort Henry was the substantial result of the effort.

And just as the recent great war in the Far East was coming to a close there was an illustration of the value a great waterway is to a nation in predominance on the sea, which scarcely seems to have been so generally noticed as it should have been. The strategical movement referred to possesses, however, an interest equal to, and as well worth our attention as, that of any other incident of the war. Nowhere is to be found a more telling illustration of the wide influence of sea-power, and it should claim the close attention of us whose chief weapon is maritime force. Just before peace was made, as will be remembered, the Japanese, having captured Saghalien, boldly directed the course of their strategy beyond Castries Bay and the Tumen, far away northwards to the mouth of the Amur. Now, if we examine a map we shall see that that great waterway in its lower course flows due north for some 400 miles from Khabarovsk to Nikolaievsk, and forms the western boundary of the maritime province. A sea-power, therefore, in command both of the river and of the sea coast, could completely isolate and cut off that valuable territory. When Linievitch was entrenching himself and preparing to make a determined stand south of Harbin, it was evident that the Japanese forces threatening Kharbarovsk from the south, acting in combination with an

SKETCH MAP OF PART OF NORTH AMERICA.

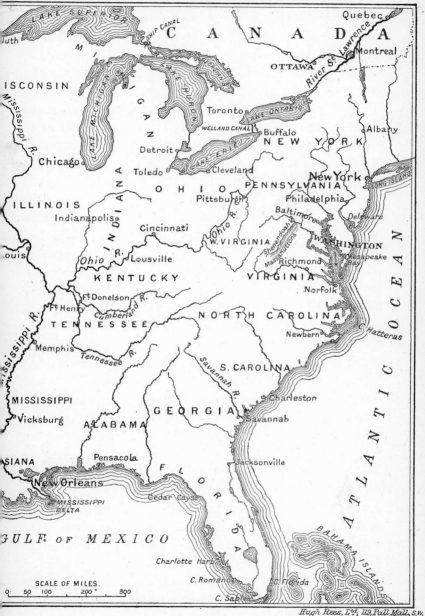

SCALE OF MILES.
0   50   100   200 *   300

Hugh Rees, L^td, 119, Pall Mall, S.W.

6

expedition up the Amur, must make him uneasy as to his rear, and must weaken his resolution. The great waterway offered a road of approach of which the Japanese were enabled by naval success to avail themselves. And in fact a naval force did appear at Nikolaievsk, created a panic amongst the inhabitants, and an expedition up the river was in progress when the armistice blossomed into peace. Because of the geographical conditions involved the arm of sea-power could stretch so far as to reach round the long front of the huge opponent. The maritime province might undoubtedly have been isolated and cut off in the manner described had the struggle continued. Thus the Japanese would have acquired a substantial slice of Russian territory—a tangible trophy which would have become invaluable when terms of peace were under discussion at the end of a more protracted war.

How difficult it has always been to strike at Russia is well recognized. Her very bulk is her safeguard; and brilliant as were the Japanese victories, they were fought at such a distance from the centres of Russian life that they were able to wrest from their opponents no portion of the empire except Saghalien. Had the war been prolonged further, the capture of Vladivostok and of the maritime province would have been, as has been shown, an enormous asset to Japan, and it is highly probable that the policy of their Government had such an enterprise in view. Here, at any rate, we have a concrete example of how a naval and military force combined may accomplish much in a region where a purely military force could not even attempt

SKETCH MAP OF
MANCHURIA
AND PARTS OF ADJOINING COUNTRIES

anything. We are once more reminded how a
great waterway facilitates combined action between
armies and ships, and, studying potentialities such

as have been indicated, we may recognize in the Amur another Mississippi and another Nile.

There are other great rivers in the Far East, and, borne on their deep waters, warships can travel hundreds of miles inland. There are mighty rivers, too, in European Russia, which as avenues of approach or channels of supply to armies, whether in defence or in attack, may possibly play a great part in the world's future.

RIVERS AS AN ASSISTANCE TO DEFENCE

The cases of great rivers coinciding with a line of advance, and thus enormously aiding sea-power, have been quoted as of the highest importance to strategy. It has also been shown how a waterway will supplement a line of communications ; but it must be pointed out that there is another side to the medal, and that a great stream has often been recognized as a powerful factor in the defence of a country, though as an indirect rather than as a direct obstacle.

Where a river is parallel to the line of advance of an enemy, fortresses or bridge-heads protecting its main passages become strategical points of much consequence, and develop the resisting power of the country to a high degree. The campaigns on the Danube and the Po during many centuries bear witness to this truth, and the Archduke Charles has declared that the history of the wars of Southern Germany prove that the valley of the Danube is the key to the country. "In all times its banks have been struggled for, and the issue of these great conflicts has always been to the advantage of the side that mastered them."[1]   Fortresses sited on a river in the circumstances under discussion are strengthened by their situation and the difficulty it imposes on their investment. They flank the line of the enemy's advance, and compel him either to stop and seize them, or weaken his army by detachments left to mask them. Vicksburg is here an example to us. We may also quote the experiences of Napoleon in 1809, when Ulm, Ratisbon, and Passau, Linz, and Krems, all strong places on the Danube, attracted each a detachment from his main army. Thus his fighting strength was eaten into, and at Aspern and Essling he was no longer strong enough to crush the Archduke Charles, but was forced to retire into an island on the Danube to gather reinforcements for a fresh effort.

JUNCTIONS OF THE RIVERS AS SITES FOR FORTRESSES

Where great waters meet is often an admirable site for a fortress. An enemy besieging or investing it has to split his force into three sections to complete the cordon of investment. Metz, situated where the Seille and Moselle unite, is a familiar illustration of this kind of stronghold, but there are many others not very far away—Coblenz, for instance, and Ehrenbreitstein, where Moselle and Rhine and Lahn mingle together ; Lyons, where Rhone and Saone are joined ; while reference to an atlas will discover further examples. In fact, it

[1] See Hamley's *Operations of War*, Blackwood, 1907, p. 282, and note the reservation in the Archduke's dictum which Hamley points out.

may be stated that the confluences of rivers with one another or with the sea have marked the sites of the most celebrated fortresses, and such points of junction often form what are known as strategical points.

STRATEGICAL POINTS

Such centres of gravity are found everywhere in a theatre of war where a locality exists the possession of which by either belligerent must mould or modify the course of operations.

The passages of great rivers are certainly important strategical points. So, too, are mountain passes, or great railway centres, or capitals of countries, or natural features which may be said to guard approaches or supply issues for advance. Forests and road junctions may similarly be strategical points, but the value of all localities will vary with the character of the opponent and the nature of the country. Thus, in savage or semi-civilized warfare, grazing tracts where cattle are accumulated may become strategical points. Water-supply in foreign regions is often a factor in creating a point of high strategical value. Even a region invested with a supernatural character, by the presence in it of revered burying-places or sacred temples, may become elevated to the status of a strategical centre.

CAPITALS

Capitals, being products of civilization, vary enormously in importance. Paris may be said to be the brain of France. Deprived of her brain the

country could not survive.   London may be termed
the heart, and equally the vital spot, of England ;
so much can scarcely be said of Berlin, and such
terms would certainly not be appropriate to Pretoria,
or to Washington or to Ottawa, although Montreal
would mean much to Canada.   Montreal is, indeed,
a place of special interest to those who study the
bearings of geography on strategy.   It is, to begin
with, situated on a mighty river, the St. Lawrence,
which is here crossed by the celebrated Victoria
Bridge, a structure two miles long, and an engineering achievement of the first importance.   The river
forms the link between an important ocean traffic
and the system of Canadian canals which leads into
the great lakes placed in the very centre of the
country.   Montreal must, therefore, by its situation,
always be a point of immense commercial importance ; but the neighbourhood which embraces the
lakes and rivers has acquired an additional value
from the existence of the great railways which
man has added to the features of nature.   As long
as Great Britain retains command of the sea, and
can preserve inviolate the canals which link the
great lakes to the St. Lawrence, she can, at any
rate, seriously dispute any claim to predominance
on those inland waters, and an American invasion
of Canada will lose much of its terrors for her.

Enterprises against the long line of the Canadian
Pacific Railway could but assume the character of
raids while the important strategic points I have
named, created by physical geography and improved
by scientific effort, remained in British hands.

On the other hand, should the United States be

able to block the canals against us, another great difficulty will be added to the vexed problem of Canadian defence.

Quebec, too, may be quoted as a strategical point of even greater importance than Montreal, because it guards the watergate of Canada, controls the St. Lawrence, and forbids the navigation of the river to all but those whom it chooses to admit. Here, again, we have a striking example of the influence of a river on strategy, and the strategical necessities which tend to create strong places on the banks of great waterways.

EXAGGERATED TERMS OFTEN USED IN STRATEGICAL DISCUSSIONS

It is in no spirit of pedantry that a word of warning is added here. Though use has been made of the word " guard," and though domination and control have been suggested in connection with the celebrated fortress just referred to, it is recommended that such terms be employed with careful discrimination when strategical geography is under discussion. Writers on military subjects are prone to indulge in violent metaphors and express themselves in exaggerated terms. Squadrons are hurled on the foe, opponents are overwhelmed, battalions are crushed, or are rent and reel before the blast of musketry, armies are driven headlong into the sea, men are trampled under-foot, and blood often flows like water. Perhaps infected by the contagion of such language, writers sometimes express themselves equally picturesquely, but inaccurately and thoughtlessly, when they speak of places which Art or Nature has strengthened exerting an influence by no means inherent in their geographical situation. The possession of a mere locality, however menacing in appearance or naturally adapted for defence, does not imply domination or command.

When people talk of the Rock of Gibraltar commanding the Straits below, it is very often apparent that they imagine that guns placed on that commanding position could destroy any vessel passing beneath. If the strategical value of Gibraltar depended only on the development of such powers, it could have been but of little importance during by far the greater part of the last 200 years, when the effective range of cannon was usually not more than a mile. Gibraltar is a strategical point of high importance because it supplies a dock and a place of refuge, and what is known as a *point d'appui* for sea-going fleets, at the gate of the Mediterranean. No nation weak at sea, even if it were allowed to possess it, would dominate anything from Gibraltar but the belt of water under the range of its cannon. We must never forget that by taking up a passive attitude of defence we dominate nothing except the glacis of our stronghold, and that no natural fortress, however strong, is usually worth anything except as a coign from which an active force may leap.

This truth is applicable not only by sea, but by land also. No better illustration of what is meant can be quoted than the story of the capture of Majuba Hill by Sir George Colley in the Boer War of 1881. That achievement could have exerted no influence on the course of his operations against the Boers, because he could get no artillery

on the top of the mountain with which to drive
his opponents from their laager and their entrenchments on Laing's Nek, while the place itself offered
him no facilities for an advance against the enemy.

A great commander, when he makes an effort to
seize such a spot, only intends to utilize it as a
stepping-stone to a further success. From one
vantage-point to the next a series of strides land
him finally in a position from whence he can
command decisive results.

Both on sea and land it would often save leaders
from a fatal error of " doing something " if they said
to themselves before they drew the plan of operations to acquire a particular spot: " How can the
enemy neutralize its loss? What shall I do with
it when I have obtained it? What shall my next
step be? The fame and moral effect of my achievement may do something morally if any revered
traditions are at stake; but, putting sentiment
on one side, what use will it be in a military
sense?" If such questions cannot be answered
satisfactorily, we may be very sure that the place
in question does not really count for much, and is
rarely in itself worth capture.

The chief geographical features which govern
the operations of war, and which should therefore
provide officers with subjects for close study, have
been but sketched, and that one to us most important of all—the Sea—has as yet been barely
mentioned. Some consideration will, therefore, now
be given to that elemental factor in success or
failure when what may be termed "world-struggles"
occupy our attention.

CHAPTER V

No nation can emerge to the highest political eminence, or hope to speak with authority in the world's council-chamber, without at least a colourable claim to mastery on the waves. The struggle between Rome and Carthage turned on sea-power. The foundation of the rule of the Cæsars was built by a battle won upon the seas. The giant growth of the Turk was arrested when the command of the Eastern Mediterranean was snatched from him. Spain, at the zenith of her power, was free of the road to the West Indies and Southern America. Now we see the greatest military power in the world endeavouring to duplicate strength on the waters with military predominance ashore. Whether this effort will be a successful one or not will depend in a large degree on geographical conditions. The development of sea-power hinges, in the first place, on physical geography, though there are other factors in its production, connected with other branches of geographical science, which must be noticed.

Some of the fauna and flora of certain countries are occasionally distinguished by unusual development, because some natural characteristic of their soil or climate fosters the growth, be it of horses or sheep or oxen, of vines or corn. Thus the limestone in the Irish soil gives bone to horses; the slopes of the Côte-d'Or produce an inimitable Burgundy; and sea-power, if not always the offspring of nature, can with difficulty reach full development unless fostered the natural advantages geography bestows.

Examine the natural features of European countries, and consider how their configuration has aided the growth of sea-power or otherwise! England is favoured by geography because her coal and iron are to be found near her coasts, and the materials for shipbuilding are, therefore, ready to hand. Great Britain and Ireland, sited as they are, obviously flank the great trade routes bearing millions of tons of valuable commerce up the Channel to the Baltic and the North Sea. But England has other natural advantages too. Her greatest natural ports are situated on her southern coast-line, and therefore their position peculiarly favours the issue forth and safety in harbour of fleets, whether of merchant vessels or men-of-war. Hydrographic conditions force deep-draught ships to pass close in front of our ports. A large proportion of the commerce of the world, measured by the value of ships and the commodities they carry, must run the gauntlet of our strongholds at short distances, especially in the English Channel. The protection of our own maritime trade and an onslaught on that of an opponent is, therefore, rendered easier for us than for some other nations, and we are indebted to geographical conditions for our advantage.   But, above all, England is an island, and her entire frontier a sea-board.   She had little or no reason to fear an invasion of her territory by surprise, and she was secure against a counter-stroke while her navy was supreme.   Her chief ambition and energies could, therefore, be devoted to the cultivation and development of maritime strength.   Since the period of the Tudors her rulers have had the good sense to dismiss from their minds any ideas of continental aggrandizement, and have wisely turned her attention towards commercial advantage and colonization.

On the other side of the Channel, that country which was long our stoutest enemy, and is now our cordial friend, while she may rival us as to position, is not so favourably endowed by Nature as regards facilities for refuge, or obstruction, or for aggression.   Again, though France has been given a seaboard extending from the Mediterranean to the Channel, and possesses a great base at Toulon, her advantage on the Mediterranean has been counteracted by the interposition of Spain between two portions of her coast; while we, for long her most formidable opponent, have seized the most important strategical point in the intervening peninsula.   The length of the French coast-line and the other natural advantages which Nature bestowed upon her have thus been marred in a manner which thwarted her efforts to create a strong sea-power, although this defect was only one of several causes responsible for the result.   The fertile fields of France had so much to offer her people that they were but little tempted to foreign adventure.   Thus her people became less adapted to a sea-going life than were those less happily circumstanced. The contiguity of neighbouring states fired the imagination of her rulers to seek wealth and glory in continental conquests. The energies of the country were not concentrated on one issue as were ours. Up to the end of the Revolutionary War, France, with a greater population than England, had more difficulty in manning her fleet. She had less reserve power because she had a smaller mercantile marine.

Spain, too, has an extensive coast-line, and Spain was once a great sea-power which has now fallen from its high estate. The presence of an English stronghold in the centre of her sea-board has been a formidable obstruction to her naval progress. There are other reasons for her decline connected with the character of Spanish colonization which we need not here discuss; but attention is drawn to this one because it is distinctly connected with geography, and is certainly not to be overlooked.

Germany, in some respects, has been favoured by geography in her maritime development. Many navigable rivers flow into the North Sea, great waterways attract and facilitate commercial dealing, and commerce is the mother of sea-power. But coal and iron are not, in her case, placed in the favourable positions wherein we come upon them in our country, and a benevolent providence has been less kind to her than to us.

" In Germany, coal and iron are not found close to the sea-coast, but have been placed by Nature far away inland in the middle and south of the country. The most important shipbuilding towns of this country are situated hundreds of miles from the principal coal and iron centres ; in fact, the average distance which the heavy German raw material has to travel overland before being worked into ships is approximately 400 miles, a distance greater than that which separates London from Glasgow. How great are Germany's difficulties owing to her unfavourable geographical position may be seen from the fact that when, in the year 1878, a Government investigation was made into the German iron industry, it was found that from 20 per cent. to 30 per cent. of the cost of production of German iron was accounted for by the cost of transport over long distances, whilst the cost of transport in respect of English iron was said to amount only from 8 per cent. to 10 per cent. of the cost."[1]

To obviate these great disadvantages the Dortmund-Ems Canal was constructed some few years ago at a cost of no less than four millions, and by this means the transportation of iron and steel to be used in shipbuilding from the interior of Westphalia to the shipyards on the North Sea and on the Baltic was materially cheapened. Similar considerations urge Germany to undertake the canalization of the Moselle, and to make it a navigable river from Metz to Coblenz, which ships of 600 tons may traverse. The ironworks of Lorraine are close to the Moselle, and the transit of minerals from the metalliferous regions of that province to the Rhine would be immensely cheapened by the suggested waterway. It is proposed, too, to canalize the Saar

[1] *Contemporary Review,* No. 483, p. 325.

as a further extension of this scheme. In a subsequent chapter further development of German waterways will be discussed.

Germany is hampered, too, by the climatic conditions of the Baltic and by the flat and shoaling character of its coast-line. Moreover, Denmark divides her sea-board, and the mouth of the Elbe is by Nature widely separated from Kiel. Therefore Germany has called in Art to rectify geography, and has dug the great ship canal which neutralizes Denmark, and links Germany's great arsenal at Kiel with the mouth of the waterway that has just been named.

Russia, with a long sea-board, has been grievously hampered by Nature. Her Baltic ports become closed by frost during many months of the year. She is at a disadvantage, too, because her great waterways flow either into frozen seas, into huge inland lakes, or into waters from which the outlet is held by a foreign Power, and therefore constitute a *mare clausum*. Thus, the Baltic, the Caspian, and the Black Sea have all offered obstacles to the progress of Russian sea-power, and she has accordingly projected the construction of a canal from Riga on the Baltic to Kherson on the Black Sea.[1] France, too, recognizing the defects of her

---

[1] The following statement appeared in the *Morning Post* of February 22, 1906 : " The Imperial Commission, presided over by General Ivanovsky, to report upon the question of a waterway between the Baltic and the Black Sea, has just decided in favour of the scheme, and the Emperor has approved the report and signed an instruction to begin the work at the earliest possible moment in order to give employment to the suffering peasantry in the region traversed. The Government will raise 290,000,000 roubles for the portion of the work involving the construction of a canal between the rivers Dnieper and Dvina. The engineering

coast-line, is considering the construction of a maritime canal through the South of France from Bordeaux to Cette on the Gulf of Lyons. We, of course, do not forget the greatest examples of these navigable canals in that already completed at Suez, and that under course of construction which will link the Pacific and the Atlantic Oceans through the Isthmus of Panama, of which something more will subsequently be said.

Italy and her maritime frontier have been lightly touched upon already. Her geographical formation and situation would at first sight seem to favour the development of sea-power. The Mediterranean has ever been the great route between East and West. Just as the trade routes to the North Sea and the Baltic skirt our shores, and glide past Plymouth and Portsmouth and Dover, the great commerce of the world flowed for long centuries along Italian coasts. But Italy's length is so divided up by mountains that her bays and inlets and the roads between them lie open to menace and attack. Moreover, taking Italian territory as a whole, she lacks physical concentration. Sicily and Italy form two sections of a kingdom which always should have been one realm, and have at last become so. But neither Corsica nor Malta fly Italy's flag, and such islands are menaces to the security of the mainland, just as Ireland, if we can imagine it in any other hands but our own, would prove a source of strategical weakness to the remainder of the United Kingdom.

---

scheme that has been approved is American, and the enterprise is backed by foreign capital."

The development of Holland as a Sea-Power, or, indeed, as a place fit for human habitation, is, however, the most remarkable. It was originally not a question of whether Holland could command the sea, but whether the sea would not dominate her. Her achievement is the triumph of man over Nature. It is, as Dr. Johnson said in another connection, not that the thing is well or ill done, but that it is done at all, that moves our admiration. Looking at the map of Holland, one wonders how land exists at all. The estuaries of her rivers resemble arms of the sea. Salt water and fresh mingle chaotically together, and submerge the land save for the infinity of little islands that peer above the deluge, while lakes and marshes are set in the firmer soil like islands in the sea. It is not a country by law of physical geography at all, but an astounding achievement of human pertinacity and energy ; created by Hollanders, it remains in existence because they watch and tend it, and when they cease doing so it will disappear. A whole army of engineers keep up an incessant contest with Nature. A struggle to confine the sea, repair and attend to dams and sluices, drain lakes and marshes, is always being carried on. Yet every year some little increment to the agricultural soil is made. The marvellous tale can be studied at length in other books ; here it is enough to say that to attribute the sea-power which Holland formerly developed so highly, and still fosters, to her geographical situation between France and the Baltic and the mouths of the great German rivers, is to do but paltry justice to a heroic race.

Adversity and the poverty of their soil hardened their character, and drove the Dutchmen to seek food in the waters. They became fishermen, and fished, too, with such success that they had soon more fish than they could consume. Therefore, they sold and exported the surplus. The fishermen were quickly traders, and in time the decline of the Italian republics allowed the trade of the Levant to fall into their hands. Holland developed into the great carrying power of the world, and her merchant navy became, as in our case, the mother of fleets.

And, be it noted, the greatness of Holland's sea-power fell because in their prosperity her people forgot her geographical history; forgot that for food and wealth she depended not on her own soil, but on her trade, and that a powerful navy was necessary to protect that trade.

INFLUENCE OF INVENTIONS ON SITES OF HARBOURS

The statesman and the soldier who would understand the effect which the construction of great canals and other achievements of the engineer may have on the course of the history of the world must study how in past times physical features have influenced operations. Some of the ambitious efforts of man will, when completed, rival the handiwork of Nature herself, and the physical geography of the world will become shaped by the calculations of a scientist. One striking example of how inventive science has modified the influence of geography is shown in the difference of considerations which now prescribe the choice of site for a commercial harbour. Formerly, the centres of commercial activity lay up an estuary or arm of the sea as far inland as possible. This was so because, in the first place, roads were bad, and the more use that could be made of water transport the better. Not only that, but the storehouses of great merchants were most safely situated at the end of a long avenue of approach, where the robbers of the ocean could only penetrate with difficulty. Accordingly we find Venice ensconcing herself at the head of the Adriatic, Constantinople protected by the narrows of the Bosphorus and the Dardanelles ; London, Antwerp, and Calcutta set deeply in great estuaries.

Now, however, that railways have largely superseded canals as a means of transport inland, it is important to continue the iron road as far as possible. Accordingly, in modern times, the ports of departure for sea-borne traffic, in place of lying at the head of inlets, are often placed at the end of promontories and peninsulas. Brindisi, for example, has supplanted Venice ; and Milford Haven, to come nearer home, has become a competitor with Bristol, although the opening of the Avonmouth Docks in 1908 may now preserve the ascendancy of the latter town. From Fishguard to Rosslare, a new route to Ireland has also lately been established. Fishguard will become the first port of call from America, and the mails from New York will reach London six hours earlier than at present.

KNOWLEDGE OF TIDES

And turning to the realm where strategy and tactics mingle together, and the prescience of a general may modify or dictate the course of fighting, other phenomena connected with maritime geography may be of help—a knowledge of the tides, for example, is often important. In certain parts of the globe the wind affects their rise and fall. A strong wind blowing from a certain direction may render places accessible, and therefore assailable, which under normal conditions can not be approached. Scipio Africanus got possession of New Carthage by applying his knowledge of such a phenomenon at that place. He assaulted the works by which the isthmus on which the city stood was defended, but this was not the spot where he intended his main effort to fall. A spot was known to him where the land breeze at ebb tide so far lowered the water of the lagoon which communicated with the sea, and bathed the foot of the walls of the stronghold on one side, that his men could walk through it. Through those shallow waters he himself led his troops, who, rearing their ladders where the besieged, little dreaming of an escalade in that part, had left the walls undefended, effected an easy entrance and made themselves masters of the place.[1]

Before the Battle of Crecy, Edward III. escaped from a critical situation by geographical knowledge —tardily gained, however, through the services of

---

[1] *Carthage and the Carthaginians*, by R. Bosworth-Smith. Longmans, London, p. 295.

a spy.   Hemmed in as he had been during the previous operations, and at his wits' end, he learned of a ford eight miles below Abbeville.   Thither he marched, and waiting till the ebb tide had lowered the waters, forced the passage, pursued his way northward through the forest of Crecy, reached the position where he faced his foes, and gained one of the most celebrated victories in our history.[1]

The great Turenne,[2] in 1658, won the celebrated battle of the Dunes, June 14, against the army of the Spanish Fronde, commanded by Don John of Austria and Condé, with whom were the Dukes of York and Gloucester, by availing himself of knowledge of a similar character. The enemy's right under Don John rested on the sea ; Turenne made a false attack upon his adversary's centre to gain time till the tide should run out, and leave an interval between the Spanish right and the waves.   Then by a rapid flank movement on the sands he turned and enveloped the enemy's position and routed his army.   Subsequently he proceeded with the siege of Dunkirk, which surrendered to him nine days later.   This battle has a special interest for us.   The Stuart Princes and their followers fought with the Spaniards.   British soldiers sent by Cromwell took part in that turning movement—the decisive stroke of the day—which has just been described. Cromwell's warships co-operated by bringing their fire to bear on the Spanish right, and thus sup-

[1] *Vide* the account in *The History of the British Army*, by the Hon. J. W. Fortescue, vol. i., book i., chap. iii., p. 33.

[2] *Turenne*, by H. M. Hozier.   Chapman and Hall, London, 1885.

ported the attack of the army ; while, finally, it was to England that Dunkirk was handed over when it fell.

Again, no operation of the Peninsular War is more worthy of study than the passage of the Bidassoa by Wellington in October, 1813, and a salient feature of that feat of arms is the passage of the river by the fords in its estuary west of the bridge. The French had every advantage that ground could give them, but they had not reckoned with the possibilities of the ebbing tide.

The list of occasions on which a particular knowledge of the sea-coast has favoured armies has not by any means been exhausted, but the penultimate example quoted finds its counterpart in an operation present to the minds of us all, also carried out by the allies of this country, and appealing, therefore, to us with special force. The example afforded by the Battle of Kinchou (May 26, 1904), when the Russians were attempting to hold back the Second Japanese Army under Oku from advancing to the siege of Port Arthur, is one that should not be overlooked. It will be remembered how the progress of the battle was uncertain, because the Japanese attack, owing to the Russian flanks extending from sea to sea, had to be a frontal one, with the proverbial disadvantages attaching to such an operation ; but the Japanese 4th Division on the Russian left, finding the water shallow, waded through it, and succeeded in storming the left of the Nanshan position and in gaining the victory. Their efforts were supplemented by the fire of four gunboats. On the other side of the peninsula the resistance of the Russians was strengthened also by the fire from a Russian warship in Talienwan Bay. In one respect this battle affords a unique example for us. It exhibits the army and navy of both combatants co-operating simultaneously on both flanks of a position, and it furnishes us, as has been said, with a salient example of how a knowledge or quick appreciation of local geographical conditions enabled one side to seize an advantage.

Has time been wasted in going back more than two thousand years in one instance, and hundreds of years in others, to make good a point? Is there any profit in setting operations carried through with magazine rifles beside others accomplished before gunpowder was invented? What basis of comparison can exist between Scipio and Oku, or even between a Plantagenet king and Turenne? The gulf of time is bridged by human nature. Personality, force of character, quickness of observation, resourcefulness win battles now, have won them, and will win them, because these qualities make leaders of men. Such leaders gain victories because they possess the sense, natural or acquired, of recognizing opportunity, of utilizing every kind of knowledge, of bending accidental circumstances to their ends. With some the sense may be latent from birth, and occasion will develop it as a match will set a lamp ablaze. Some see for themselves what others only see when they are told how and where to look. But the less gifted may acquire by practice and study a second-hand experience that will often produce a substitute for the congenital faculty. It is because they

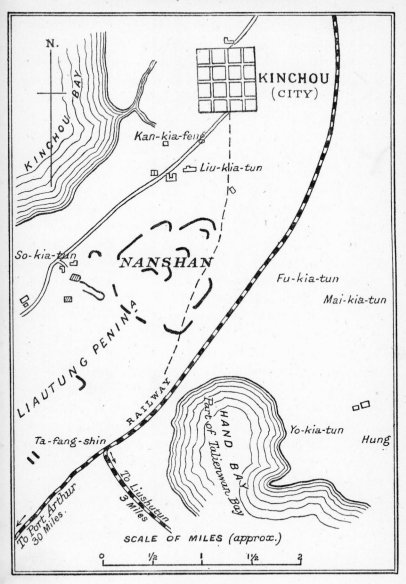

SKETCH MAP

BATTLE OF KINCHOU, May 26th, 1904.

Hugh Rees, Ltd., 119, Pall Mall, S.W.

stir the imagination that Military History and Geography are so valuable to the soldier, enlarge his horizon, and foster military instinct. We cannot profit by one without a knowledge of the other, and some of the most difficult problems that puzzle generals are in their essence geographical.

CHAPTER VI

LINES OF COMMUNICATION

SUCCESS or failure in war ultimately hinges on communications. That side which can stay the longest—that is to say, which continues to be fed and supplied and reinforced with regularity—will at length emerge victorious. Communications spell strategy, and it is generalship or strategy that wins wars, though it is possible for courage and skill at arms to win battles, or even campaigns. When armies depended on supplies drawn laboriously over long miles in cumbrous waggons, and men struggled forward on foot to the armies they were to reinforce, water communications were immeasurably superior to any roads and paths. Until quite lately ships supplied a means of communication and supply superior to those that railways could furnish, and the potency of sea-power had a significance almost unchallenged where transport all over the globe was in question.

The recent Russo-Japanese War has, however, amongst its other surprises, brought the potency of trans-Continental railways very much to the front. Modern rail-power had never been pitted against sea-power, in so marked a degree, as during

that war, and its achievements have invested
transport by rail with an importance disquieting in
relationship to that by sea.   When the war closed,
Russia had been able to collect nearly a million of
men in the field at the end of a single line of rail
more than 5,000 miles away from Moscow.   The
feat was marvellous, and if Japan could rival Russia,
she did so at only six days' journey from her
home base.   Previous to the war with Japan, the
fragile nature of Russia's communications was the
main argument against the chances of her success.
There was only a limited quantity of rolling-stock,
and locomotives ; the return of empty carriages and
trucks on a single line would impose inevitable and
damaging delays.   Locomotives must be cleaned,
and could only work a certain number of hours at
a stretch.   The permanent way was insufficiently
ballasted ; the rails only weighed 18 pounds to the
foot-run.

So ran the far-stretched chain of difficulties, the
vast web of a thousand technical objections.   It
was remembered how, in 1877-1878, Russia had only
beaten the Turks by dint of supreme exertions,
because she did not possess the command of the sea,
and her forces, numbering hundreds of thousands,
had to be fed and supplied by means of a single line
of rail, and that, too, with the gauge broken at
Oungheni on the frontier.   The soft alluvial deposits
of the Danube Valley were then the strongest allies
of the Turks.   Was Russia to overcome Japan with
only a single line of rail behind her, and that stretched
over distances which were represented by thousands
of miles, while those of 1877 were only to be reckoned

by hundreds ? The energy and talent of Count Khilkoff gradually changed pessimism into doubt, and doubt into acknowledgment of success. The railway did wonders, but it foreshadowed wonders greater still. What might not the future have in store if the unprepared present could do so much ? More lines of rails, improved laying of rails, better stations, more convenient rolling-stock, all the numberless products of more fully-developed science, working with a definite object in view, will some day enhance the powers of the railroad far beyond what they were a few years back. We may have to reconsider some of our articles of faith in the near future, and already must part with some time - honoured formulas. For the present, however, transport by rail is far more expensive than transport by sea. Freight to the Far East by rail is £3 per ton, by sea only £2 a ton. The cost is therefore 50 per cent. in England's favour, if everything were to be sent from England and Russia. But, as a matter of fact, England can tap markets nearer to the Far East and cheaper than those at home, while Russia cannot. Moreover, sea-power remains essential to dominion beyond the seas, and endows its possessors with the power of despatching expeditions as raids or invasions to the territories of their opponents, and permits them to make diversions or counter-attacks that did, and still in certain countries may, prove most effective efforts of strategy. It is when the selection of the scene of such expeditions is considered that military geography is of the greatest help to statesmen and generals.

Let us consider first the question of an invasion intended as a diversion. Unless the invader strikes at some point of such strategic importance that the enemy will be compelled to turn upon him in strength, his diversion will have accomplished little. Indeed, unless the arrival of the invader's expedition offers a menace sufficient to draw more troops from the main struggle than have been withdrawn to make the counterstroke, the strategy of diversion will have failed.

Neither will it be more successful if the enemy, who will be working on interior lines, can, by means of good railway connections, concentrate his troops rapidly, despatch superior forces to meet and crush the invasion, and then bring them back to the spot where the main struggle may be expected to occur.

In other words, the success or failure of a diversion or counterstroke hinges, so far as Continental warfare is concerned, on the excellence or otherwise of the inland railway communications of the country assailed. It follows that, since all European Powers are now well furnished with railway systems, and have enormous masses of men at command, it will be more difficult than it used to be for any force these islands can place on board ship to produce substantial effect in a Continental struggle.

The Crimean War ultimately turned—as it has been shown wars must turn—on efficiency of communications. Sea-transport was then pitted against road-transport, and that, too, owing to climatic conditions, of inefficient type. One battalion which marched in full strength from Moscow in 1854 is said to have reeled into Sebastopol with only thirteen men in the ranks. Miles and miles of snow and slush; hunger, fever, frost-bite, had done their work. We emerged victorious under such conditions because the sea offered better roads than any the enemy could utilize. But now, when the Russian troops in Sebastopol are connected by rail with the heart of the Russian Empire, huge numbers could be poured in to reinforce those in the fighting-line were we again to assail that stronghold, and while our difficulties would be much the same, the task of our opponents would be far less exacting than was the case fifty years ago.

It appears, in fact, that to invade the European possessions of an opponent does not in these days offer much prospect of success.

We should rather seek to impose upon our opponent the difficulties and disadvantages long lines of communications, whether by land or sea, bring with them, and force him to fight at some distance from his home. The ideal thing to do would be to strike him at some valued possession connected with the heart of his empire by water only. For in that case, if our sea-power prove as formidable as we have a right to expect it to be, he will have to meet us where our difficulties were at a minimum, while his were at their greatest.

The question, however, would then arise, whether the colony across the seas which we attacked would be of such importance that the enemy would feel his prestige vitally involved in retaining it; whether its loss would be such a reverse as would make him sue for peace; or whether he could afford to let the colony go without visible loss of moral or material force. It would become necessary to examine the objective selected from the broadest geographical standpoint, scrutinizing its resources, wealth, commerce, and political importance most minutely, before an answer could be given. The loss of Cuba, although it did not add to her material wealth, affected Spanish pride so closely as to cause her to defend it at all hazards. We could not afford to let India or Australia go until exhaustion prostrated us. France would set equal store on the retention of Algeria, but Russia and Germany have few remote possessions associated with strong national sentiment, and are less open to serious assault by sea.

It has been thought right to draw attention to the difficulties that modern civilization has imposed upon a policy of invading hostile territories ; but that in certain cases they may, and will, be undertaken in the future by a nation with such a wide field of action as ours is sure. And wherever and whenever they are undertaken, certain strategical conditions, all of which lie within the realm of geography, must first be satisfied.

The tactical and geographical conditions must be carefully considered, and, with regard to them, most cordial co-operation between naval and military commanders must be established. The nature of the coast, the depth of water, the local peculiarities of the spot, the weather, the tides, the usually prevailing wind, the probability of fogs,[1]

---

[1] Writing from Sebastopol on March 3, 1855, to Lord Panmure, Lord Raglan said : " As the season of the fogs in the Black Sea is approach-

will all affect the plans of the naval commander, and it is he, at this early stage, who must be the supreme authority.   A disembarkation on a hostile shore must come as a surprise to be successful nowadays.   A surprise premises an open beach ; an open beach is often associated with surf.   Surf has baffled many an effort to land troops in such a situation.   Lord Wolseley has told us that the General who leaves surf out of his calculations is a gambler.

The landing at Aboukir Bay in 1801 was delayed for five days owing to the weather.   A similar delay was encountered when Sir John Moore's expedition landed in Portugal in 1808.   The French expedition to Algiers in 1830 was held up by the weather for an even longer time.

A covering position to ward off interference with the tedious process of disembarkation has to be found ; jetties, to facilitate landing impedimenta and perhaps men, have also to be built.

We shall need good roads or water-ways leading from the shore into the heart of the hostile territory, in order that our channels of supply may be open and free.   We need not here enter into a detailed account of all that has to be thought of and provided for. It will be obvious from the few hints here given that army and navy will be engaged elbow to elbow, that geography, strategy, and tactics must walk hand-in-hand, and that sea and land Services must make their duties dovetail in and out.

Perhaps the most interesting examples of the

---

ing, we must take care to keep an abundance of supplies here."—
Panmure Papers, Hodder and Stoughton, London, 1908, vol. i., p. 95.

influence of geography on strategy are to be found in cases of combined action between navy and army, and more especially in those which illustrate the operation of a change of base. Napoleon has alluded to this operation as one calling forth the highest skill and offering the greatest results to a General. In our own case, sea-power endows us with a power in this respect, which is undoubtedly one of the most valuable of our military assets, not only in achieving victory, but in warding off disaster. Not infrequently has a British force been snatched from destruction by the intervention of the friendly ships, which appeared at the right moment and carried it beyond the clutches of an overbearing foe. The sea-coast parallel or behind their line of operations has often been perilous to armies. " Between the devil and the deep sea " is a proverb much respected by commanders. But to an army which has sea-power to support it the waves usually have few terrors, and often none, although the process of re-embarking from an open beach must always remain a most hazardous undertaking.

Not seldom has a British commander baffled the strategy of his opponent by an elusive change of communications arrived at by the aid of a fleet accompanying by sea the progress of the force on shore. Just as Cromwell had clung to the east coast for his supplies during the Scottish campaign of 1650, so Wellington, as he pressed his advance nearer and nearer to the French frontier, drew his supplies from the successive bases established for him by the navy along the coast. In 1815, also,

Wellington had alternate bases, and, if cut off from Ostend, could have established connections with Antwerp, or, if necessary, with ports even farther to the east. The Virginian campaigns of the American War of Secession offer many examples of how sea-power facilitates a change of base, and during the operations of Grant in 1864 its power in this respect is well illustrated. Lord Wolseley, in 1882, by the aid of the navy, is enabled to strike a brilliant stroke of strategy, and, with a swiftness and secrecy most baffling to his opponent, can suddenly transfer his transports and store-ships from Alexandria to the Suez Canal.

Sir John Moore falls back from the menace of Napoleon, and his force ultimately slips away from Corunna by aid of the transports which sea-power carried to meet the retreating columns. Massena, forcing Wellington back upon Lisbon, forgot sea-power, and imagined he was driving his foe to destruction ; whereas the lines of Torres Vedras and the geographical features of the spot secured the great Duke from calamity, and would have enabled him to escape altogether under cover of the fortifications of St. Julian on the estuary of the Tagus, had fortune gone against him.

Without having by any means exhausted the whole question, enough, perhaps, has been said to show that sea-power not only enables a naval commander to reap the advantages that geographical conditions may have placed at his disposal, but allows both the land and sea forces of a nation to act in combination, and its whole armed strength to be brought to bear. Advantages so pronounced and far-reaching have often proved decisive in the past. They have built up the greatness of States and empires, and it is to them that we owe the commanding position which we occupy in the world to-day.

Nevertheless, an intelligent appreciation of the resources of certain regions of the world, and of the means by which they may be turned to account, has in recent years brought a force into the political arena whose might may prove eventually more compelling, more irresistible, and more permanent in its results than that of sea-power itself. Slow, unobtrusive, silent, the gradual expansion of a nation is as resilient as the waves of the sea, as inevitable and forceful as the rising tide itself. Unobserved, it ebbs to and fro; progress is perhaps only noticeable when measured by the standard of years; but it forges ahead none the less.

The natural multiplication of a race, expressed in colonization, is the greatest power in the world. Progress in the science of railway constructon has lately given this force an impetus which has rendered it more potent than ever. A thousand keels, carrying tens of thousands of tons of men, of horses, of stores, plough the waves and touch at distant shores, yet a few years after every trace of a great expedition has disappeared. Headstones and half-obliterated trenches are all that are left to show that we ever occupied the plains of the Crimea. Our footprints even in South Africa are fast vanishing, while our expeditions to Syria, to Copenhagen, to Port Mahon, even to Spain, have left no traces behind them.

Sea-power, in fact, is a ferry, but a railway forms a permanent bridge. Along the line of rails cultivation and homesteads, villages and markets spring up. The steam-engine draws emigration behind it, and the home frontiers are pushed farther and farther outwards as the colonists clear and dig. Geographical boundaries are gradually obliterated or modified as the resources of districts are better appreciated and understood. The virgin soil or mineral wealth of wild regions is then exploited, until, little by little, the face of the country changes in a manner suggestive of the operations of natural phenomena. A force resembling that of Nature herself is silently enlisted into the ranks of a potential invader, and the work of the plough and spade may prove in the long-run as effective as that of the gun and bayonet.

The rough sketch which follows shows the progress railway construction has made from West to East. The emigrants and goods-waggons, or the troop-trains and their trucks with guns and stores that may take their place, may now be carried from the heart of Europe to the shores washed by the waters of the Pacific.

A similar diagram illustrates the even more marvellous growth of railway communication in Canada and the connection that has been established by the metal lines between the Western Atlantic and the Eastern Pacific.

The Dominion of Canada two years ago had a network of railways 21,518 miles in length, all of 4 feet 8½-inch gauge. The Canadian Pacific line from Montreal to Vancouver is 2,906 miles in

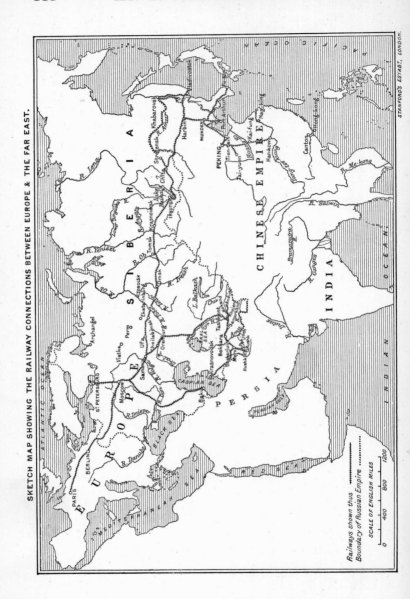

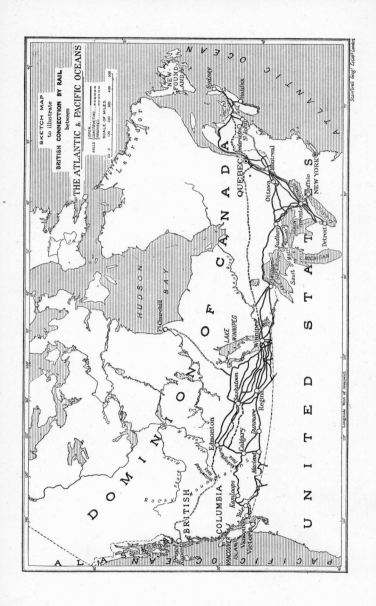

SKETCH MAP
to illustrate
BRITISH CONNECTION BY RAIL
between
THE ATLANTIC & PACIFIC OCEANS

RAILS { OPEN
CONSTRUCTING
PROPOSED

SCALE OF MILES
100 50 0 100 200 300 400 500

length.   The traveller who avails himself of this railway, and a line of Pacific steamers subsidized by the Imperial Government and that of the Dominion, can reach Yokohama from Montreal in fourteen days.

The total area of Canada is 3,619,818 square miles.   Her population in 1901 was 5,371,315.

As an illustration of the working of economical forces under favourable geographical conditions such as we have been discussing, we may note what is going on before our very eyes to-day in the case of Siberia.   Time was when many of us thought of Siberia as a half-forgotten region of the world, bound with frost and snow most of the year, where a few miserable exiles dragged out a precarious existence.   No fate evoked more heartfelt sympathy than that of the exile relegated to that " realm of unrelenting gloom."   Recent facilities for travel and the acquisition of knowledge have, nevertheless, taught us that, however repellent part of Siberia really is, as a whole it is by no means a land of despair, although, no doubt, a country where luxury is not to be sought for, and where hardihood must be possessed by those who would inhabit it. On the other hand, there is an enormous agricultural capacity in the land ; mineral wealth abounds, and there are huge areas of soil not inferior in any way to those of the Canadian North-West, or of Southern Russia.

In the European provinces of Russia there are thousands and hundreds of thousands of sturdy, vigorous peasants who would willingly seek their fortunes in such a country.   Two obstacles, until recently, stood in their way.   The first of course was due to difficulties of transport, the second to the persistent opposition to emigration of the Russian Government, which regarded a redundant population at home as a means of securing cheap labour. In consequence, the emigration up to 1906 did not much exceed 100,000 a year.   In that year, however, the Russian Government removed its restrictions.   Since then the results have been indeed astonishing.[1]   During the first ten months in 1907 the number of emigrants rose to 556,000.   It was expected to reach a million in 1908.

According to recent statistics, the population of Russia is annually increasing at the rate of 2,500,000.   It now stands at about 150,000,000.   In twelve years' time, if the rate be kept up, it will have reached 180,000,000 ; and in 1950 more than 250,000,000.   It will then exceed the present combined population of Germany, France, Austria, Great Britain, and Italy.   The Russians are very largely an agricultural people, but they are ignorant, and unable to get the most out of the land.   Consequently a waste of land resources in European Russia exists, a scarcity of land supervenes, and the population are prone to emigrate. We may, therefore, expect the enormous number of emigrants of last year to be continued for some considerable time to come, and transportation will assist them in a manner far beyond what has been done in the past, when only a single track of railway led eastwards from Samara.

[1] *Vide* article by a correspondent of the *Times,* writing from St. Petersburg, August 5, 1908.

The earlier emigrants sent back encouraging reports of how virgin soil of about forty acres could be obtained without any of the restrictions the neighbourhood of large landed proprietors in Russia imposed upon the tenant. Pasture for cattle can be had in abundance. Soil, in no way inferior to the best in South Russia, will yield a rich harvest. A little trouble will overcome difficulties that have hitherto existed as to water. Meanwhile, rivers are full of fish, woods supply game, and as much timber as the emigrant fancies can be felled for firewood or building purposes. It is not to be wondered at that applications to emigrate have grown in volume, and that the difficulty is to keep pace with them.

A large expanse of territory, bounded by the line of railway as far as the River Ob to the north, the course of that river to the east, the Altai range to the south, and the Urals to the west, is the favourite resort. But the Government has other equally large and attractive regions for colonization to dispose of. From the Altais to Turkistan there stretches a great tract of pasture-land vaguely described as the Kirghiz Steppes, and officially known as the regions of Akmolinsk, Semi-Palatinsk, Semiretchensk, the home of the semi-nomad Kirghiz tribes, who are a race of horse-breeders. Further east lies the extensive stretch of the Yenissei basin, forming the provinces of Yenisseisk and Irkutsk. Beyond are the basins of the Amur and the Ussuri, and the Primorsk or Maritime Province. Even then the list of potential colonies is not exhausted. The first-named and westernmost area, ten years ago, was a dreary expanse of rich black soil, lying fallow.   One looked for long miles over monotonous stretches of virgin forest, devoid of any sign of human habitation except in the neighbourhood of the straggling villages, which stretched interminably along the high road in a dreary street of wooden huts.   Even here there were few signs of agriculture.   Horses and cattle supplied the staple industry.   Now the railway is bordered by strips of upturned soil.   There are attempts at irrigation, and small herds of cattle graze on the prairies. Villages are springing up on the banks of the rivers, too, with a rapidity that the official maps cannot overtake, and stone houses are replacing wooden ones in them.   But roads are still few, and consequently the swarm of emigrants cling to the railway and the rivers, while the intermediate country is deserted.

The climate is found sufficiently good by those who live there.   The winter is severely cold, but it is dry and free from winds.   Summer follows quickly on the winter months, and summer and autumn are often quite hot.   The range of the Altai Mountains is dry and invigorating, and provides pleasant health resorts.

The soil in the northern part of the square we have named consists of rich black soil yielding good crops.   The rest of the land affords excellent pasture, especially along the river valleys.   Gold and copper are found in the southern part.

The resources of the provinces at present less explored, less well known, and less thickly colonized, are certainly not inferior to those described.   The spread of Russian colonization can be continued eastward till the sea is touched. It is impossible to say how far political and economic circumstances will stimulate or retard the flow of emigration during the coming years ; but it appears probable, in view of the liberal tendencies asserting themselves in Russia and the obvious political advantages to be gained by the absorption of Eastern Asia, that the movement of emigration will continue and increase. In Russia forces are said to draw men eastwards, as formerly in America they drew men to the west. As more land comes under cultivation, and as methods of agriculture improve, the harvest will grow richer and richer. Siberia will become self-contained. Railways, gradually creeping eastwards, will draw the Russian people with them, and Russia, based in Siberia, will push her communications down the course of the Amur to the north-east extremities of Asia. In place of calling masses of men over 5,000 miles away by rail to the front, it will then only be necessary to draft reinforcements from the regions west of Lake Baikal—but 700 miles from the Manchurian frontier—and feed and arm them from centres a few days by rail from the battlefields of the future.

Thus, natural resources, colonization, and the building of railway communications, may alter the whole aspect of a future war.

In Russian progress, geographical conditions and strategy go hand-in-hand. Her advance, even when the ruthless measures of Yermoloff in the Caucasus and the bloodshed in Central Asia are

SKETCH MAP SHOWING RAILWAYS IN THE FAR EAST.

RAILWAYS CONSTRUCTED ┼┼┼┼┼┼┼┼   UNDER CONSTRUCTION ─ ─ ─ ─ ─ ─

Lake Baikal
R. Vitim
R. Selenga
Verkhni Udinsk
R. Szenga
R. Chilok
CHITA
R. Onon
Raidolovo
STANOVOI MOUNTAINS
Kuenga
Nerchinsk
Stretensk
R. Argun
R. Shilka
Nogodon
Pirovska
Urga
Kerulen R.
Manchuria
Dalai Nor
Hailar
R. Amur
AMUR PROVINCE
R. Ur
R. Zeya
R. Zeya
Aigun
BLAGOVESHCHENSK
Mergen
Great Bira
R. Burea
R. Amur
Khabarovsk
Nikolaievsk
Gulf of Tartary
SAGHALIEN I.
SEA OF OKHOTSK

MONGOLIA
DESERT
MANCHURIA
R. Nonni
Tsitsihar
R. Sungari
Grafskaya
R. Ussuri
Bikin
PRIMORSK
Straits of La Perouse

Sin-tchan
Harbin
Hailin
Ninguta
Muravieff Amursky
Ussuri
Spasskaya
Chernigovka
Nikolsk
YESO I.
Otaru
Mororan
Hakodate
Tsugaru Channel

Kuan-cheng-tzu
KIRIN
Kung-chu-lung
Ssu-pinoka
Grodekov
Pogranitchniya
VLADIVOSTOK
Aomori
Morioka
Akita

Liao-Ho
Fakumen
Chang-tu
Sin-min-tun
MUKDEN
Taitszu Ho
Liao-yang
Tumen R.
SEA OF JAPAN
Sendai
Yamagata
Niigata
Nikko

Kalgan
Hoang-Ho
Kin-chow
G. of Liao-tung
Newchang
Siong-chin
Won-san (Gen-san)
Nagano
Kanazawa
TOKIO
Yokosuka

PEKING
Tien-tsin
Dalny
Port Arthur
Korea Bay
Chinampo
Ping-hai
Yalu R.
KOREA
Matsu-saki
Nagoya
Yokohama

TAI-YUEN
Wei-hai-wei
Chemulpo
SEOUL
Hong-chu
Kioto
Ujiyamada

TSI-NAN
Pochan
Kiao-chow
Kaio-chow
Masampo
Fu-san
Tsushima
Hiroshima
Okayama
JAPAN
HONDO
Osaka
Wakayama

CHINA
Jameiseno
Taokow
KAI-FUNG
Honan
Hoang-Ho
GRAND CANAL
YELLOW SEA
Mokpo
KOREA STRAIT
Ishikina
Moji
Shimonoseki
SIKOK I.

Quelpart I.
Sasebo
Nagasaki
KIUSHIU I.
PACIFIC OCEAN

Kagoshima

NAN-KING
I-chang
Han-kow
Yang-tse-kiang
Shang-hai

0 100 200 300 ENGLISH MILES

London : Hugh Rees, Ltd.

STANFORD'S ESTAB?., LONDON.

kept in memory, has never had the ordered impetus
of an invasion ; her policy has been to plan the slow
absorption rather than the capture of a province,
its colonization and cultivation being steadily
adjusted to assist a further advance. The theatre
of war is prepared before the foot of a soldier
treads it. How Siberia has been, and will be,
enormously benefited by the construction of the line
of rail has been just described. As regards both
corn-growing and cattle-raising, she has an already
high commercial value. She has also vast wealth
in timber, and she produces gold, coal, and copper,
and other minerals. She lacks good communications alone, and this want it is which has hitherto
retarded her progress. When she has been colonized
this will be remedied, she herself will supply communications to more distant provinces, and form a
base of operations for military enterprises that in
the late war had to draw their resources from the
heart of Russia. It has been said[1] that the area
available for profitable settlement in Siberia is probably 2,000,000 square miles, or six times the size
of Manchuria—a region sufficient to nourish some
100,000,000 Russians. This great area does not include 2,500,000 square miles of inhospitable soil
north of latitude 65°, which, although continuously
frozen, except during a brief summer, are capable
of supporting many more millions devoted to such
pursuits as cattle-raising, mining, lumbering, and
hunting. The writer just quoted tells us that, in
spite of the barrenness of their soils, the Govern-

[1] *The Coming Struggle in Eastern Asia,* by B. L. Putnam Weale,
p. 259.

ments of Yakutsk and Yeniseisk already contain 1,500,000 souls.

Lumbering and mining on a very large scale will lead to the building of railways, and their construction will have the same effect as always amongst vigorous populations : towns and villages will spring up along the line ; new centres will be formed ; little by little fresh communities will be created, with wide aspirations and keen activities. The Trans-Siberian Railway and the feeders it will gradually throw out from it will become granaries, which will feed not only civilized populations, but may supply the huge armies of the future, when their proximity to the theatre of war calls upon them to do so. In fact, the vigorous and natural vitality of the Russian people is now being given an opportunity of spreading and expanding in a fashion that will enable Russia to realize, in the future, the ambitions she has, as yet, been unable to fulfil.

Nothing can stop the Russian landslip from ultimately overwhelming China, except China herself. To discuss whether she possesses, or ever is likely to possess, the necessary resources to resist it or not would take us far. But that Japan realizes what the development of potential Russian communications means is evident from her recent opposition to the building of a railway from Sinmin-tun to Fakumen. The pretext, no doubt, is that it will unfairly compete with the line from Mukden and Harbin. But that danger is of small strategical or commercial importance compared to the effect of an extension of the line from Fakumen to Tsitsihar, by which a considerable corner from the existing line would be cut off, and the Russians would be given, should they seize it, as they would in the event of war, a double line of advance and communication by rail into Manchuria. On the sketch map attached to this chapter the existing railways are shown in continuous lines, and that one constituting the danger against which Japan has to guard is dotted.

CHAPTER VII

CANALS AND WATER-WAYS

THE projects as regards canals and water-ways already mentioned are but the precursors of others now being undertaken or foreshadowed in European countries and across the Atlantic.

Austria a few years ago proposed a scheme of canal construction which involved an outlay of £31,900,000, out of which total, by 1912, £10,650,000 will have been expended on works now in hand. Vast sums have already been spent on the water-ways of France, and in 1903 £11,750,000 was allotted for the construction of canals and harbours.

Germany opened the Oder and Spree Canal in 1891, the Emperor William Canal in 1895, the Ems and Dortmund Canal in 1899, and the Elbe and Trave Canal in 1900. Money for the widening and deepening of the Kiel Canal has lately been granted. Recent activity in commerce and industry have greatly increased, and have urgently called for improvement in the means of transport. The provision of artificial water-ways has become the object of imperative demand. Great manufacturing centres in the Rhine Provinces and

Westphalia have sprung up, grown, and developed ; have created a traffic that has exceeded the capacity of the railway to transport ; have called for raw material in greater quantity than can be conveyed on trucks.   In these great centres water-ways, to supplement the efforts of the railway, have been demanded, and they have, in consequence, made their appearance.

In the year 1904, entirely owing to the personal exertions, it is said, of the Emperor William II., the scheme of the so-called Midland Canal—the fruit of long previous study and investigation—was submitted by the Prussian Government to the Landtag.   The object of this great undertaking was to utilize existing canals as far as possible, and to unite the upper waters of the four rivers, Rhine, Ems, Weser, and Elbe, by cutting the canal through the territory between Dortmund, Hanover, and Magdeburg.   It was further proposed to canalize the Lower Oder, and thus provide for navigation between Berlin and Stettin.   Means of intercommunication and transport in the eastern part of the kingdom were also to be extended by the improvement of the water-ways between the Oder and the Weichsel (or Vistula), and adapting these rivers themselves to navigation.   Political difficulties, however, stood in the way.   The Conservative party have been opposed to the construction of canals, and hostile to the whole scheme, because they are of opinion that reduction in the costs of transport would be injurious to the interests of agriculture.   The Opposition succeeded in causing the Government to withdraw the most

9

important parts of their proposals, and that part of the Midland Canal to be constructed between Hanover and the Elbe—that is to say, the larger half of the scheme—was dropped. With respect to the plans for improving navigation between Berlin and Stettin, no great changes were introduced, and the project, as finally sanctioned on April 1, 1905, by the Upper Chamber, comprised the following undertakings :

. 1. A canal from the Rhine to the Weser ;

2. A great navigable channel between Berlin and Stettin ;

3. The improvement of the water-way between the Oder and the Weichsel (or Vistula) ; and

4. The canalization of the Upper Oder.

The Berlin correspondent of the *Times*, writing in January, 1908, informed us that the Rhine and Weser Canal will extend from the Rhine near Dortmund to Hanover, and will be adapted for vessels of 600 tons burden. The undertaking comprises the construction of a new section of canal, 24·8 miles in length, from Dortmund to the Rhine, extending from Ruhrort to Dortmund, together with a side-canal. Additions and alterations are also to be made to the canal between Dortmund and the Ems, and provision is also made for a third section, the Ems and Weser Canal, leading from the Dortmund and Ems Canal to Hanover. The total expenditure contemplated for the entire scheme of the Rhine and Weser Canal, including the side-canal above mentioned, amounts to £12,537,500.

The navigable water-way between Berlin and

Stettin is stated in the Government memorandum to have for its object the support of Stettin in its contest with the free towns of Hamburg and Lübeck for the trade of the Elbe territory and the province of Brandenburg. It is to be noted that, owing to the construction of the Kaiser Wilhelm Canal and the canal from the Oder to the Spree, Hamburg is constantly gaining a more commanding position in those parts of the country which, in consequence of their geographical position, would appear to depend upon Stettin for their outlet to the sea. Moreover, owing to the construction of the Elbe and Trave Canals, circumstances have been in a similar way highly favourable to the development of the trade of Lübeck at the expense of Stettin. To secure the means for navigation between Berlin and Hohensaaten, a canal is projected capable of allowing the passage of vessels of 600 tons, in place of the present barges of only 170 tons burden. The construction of this waterway will, it is estimated, entail an expenditure of £2,150,000.[1]

The third scheme, which deals with the improvement of the navigation eastward from the Oder, will render it possible to employ vessels carrying 400 tons in these canals.

For all these great undertakings the sum of £16,737,500 has been voted, but this represents an outlay of capital on reproductive works which in the future will render considerable benefits to German commerce and industry.[2]

[1] *Vide* Berlin Correspondent in the *Times*, January 1, 1908.
[2] *Ibid.*

The growth of water-ways is noticeable in other parts of the world, however, besides Europe. In 1903 the State of New York decided upon the expenditure of about $21,200,000 on the construction and expansion of the inadequate Erie Canal, in order to render it available for vessels of 1,000 tons burden. In the United States the Board of Engineers of the United States Rivers and Harbours Commission, which has been investigating the question, reported at the end of 1906 that a 14-foot water-way, between St. Louis and Lockport, Illinois, can be built for $51,500,000. It is yet to be determined whether the expenditure of such a sum is warranted by the need for a deep canal. Another project which has been set on foot is that brought forward by the " Lakes to the Gulf Deep Water Association," to provide a navigable water-way from Chicago, via St. Louis, to New Orleans. The water necessary for the canals on this system is to be supplied by the Chicago Drainage Canal. A company has also been formed for the purpose of arranging for the construction of a navigable water-way between Boston Harbour and Fall River, Massachusetts. The South Sault Ste. Marie Ship Canal is, also, being provided with a new lock.

But a scheme greater than these is in contemplation. It was reported at the end of 1907 that the next important enterprise which the Canadian Government would undertake would be the Georgian Bay Canal, by which it is proposed to connect Lakes Huron and Superior with the Atlantic. First mooted some fifty years ago, the project seems now in a fair way to be realized.[1] That Canadian produce should be transported cheaply and conveniently through Canadian territory, to Canadian ports for shipment abroad, has long been the dream of Canadians. They naturally attach the greatest importance to winning for their own country the immense transport trade which has been created already, and is still growing greater every day. The extraordinary development in the trade upon the Great Lakes between 1894 and 1906 taxed to their utmost capacity the railways serving the North-West and the port accommodation on the lakes. The total freight tonnage passing through the American and Canadian locks at Sault Ste. Marie rose from 13,195,860 tons in 1894 to 51,751,080 tons in 1906. Wheat alone rose from 34,869,483 bushels in 1894 to 84,271,358 bushels in 1906, and iron ore from 6,548,876 tons in 1894 to 35,357,042 tons in 1906.[2] Such an expansion of trade demanded a corresponding increase in lake shipping, and lake steamers have consequently grown in size up to 10,000 tons, while the capital now sunk in that shipping is said to be upwards of £25,000,000. Yet only a comparatively small part of this enormous traffic passes through Canada. The ore is shipped almost entirely through Ameri-

---

[1] "Sir Wilfrid Laurier stated at Hull last night that, if the country's revenue continued to increase at the present rate, the construction of the Georgian Bay Canal would be begun immediately after the completion of the Transcontinental Railway. The estimated cost of the work necessary for a navigable channel 20 feet in depth is £19,000,000." —*Times*, October 3, 1908.

[2] *Vide* an article by a correspondent in the *Times*, December 25, 1907, from which the account has been taken.

can ports, and only 8 per cent. of the grain passes through Montreal for shipment.

The growth of the lake trade, the expansion that must follow the construction of the Grand Trunk Pacific line, and the further extension of the Canadian Pacific Railway, also call for further facilities for transport from west to east. If the mineral wealth of the northern slopes of Lake Superior and the district to the north of the Ottawa River prove anything like what Canadian geologists expect them to be, the Ottawa Valley, aided by cheap water transit and by the generation of electricity by water-power, is certain to become a most flourishing industrial centre. Reference to the map will show that by the proposed route from Georgian Bay along the French River, Lake Nipissing, and the smaller lakes through Mattawa and the Ottawa River to the St. Lawrence, and thence to the ocean, the distance is much shorter than that by way of Detroit and Buffalo to Montreal, and it is contended that it will also be much more economical.

The canal is to be 425 miles long and to have thirty-eight locks. The first of these locks at the junction of Georgian Bay and the French River is to be 594 feet above sea-level; the second, in the French River, at the height of 617 feet; and the third, from the French River to Lake Nipissing, is to raise vessels to 640 feet. From Lake Nipissing vessels will pass by way of Trout Lake and Talon Lake into the Mattawa River, whence they will descend into the Ottawa River, finally reaching the St. Lawrence River level below Montreal.

The advocates of the canal point to the natural advantages which this route possesses when compared with those of similar undertakings. Canal routes are open to serious disadvantages ; steamers have to pass through them at reduced speeds because the wash created by going fast inflicts damage on the artificial banks. The narrowness of the channel prevents steamers from passing each other under way ; one must stop to let its neighbour pass. Sidings to admit of passing have also, in most cases, to be constructed. The Georgian Bay Canal largely runs through deep-water lakes and avoids all these difficulties therefore.

The locks practically become the only hindrances to free navigation, and in practice the disadvantages inherent in an artificial canal hardly exist at all. On the other hand, the whole length is a deep water channel, well protected, and having the advantage over lake navigation that it is not exposed to storms, and that ships cannot be delayed by the weather.

The canal originally began at St. Anne's above Montreal, and passing through Ottawa and Mattawa Rivers, crossed Talon, Turtle, and Trout Lakes. The canal there reached the summit level, 659 feet above the level of the St. Lawrence at Montreal. A short cut across the summit about five miles long carried the canal into Lake Nipissing, and thence by the French River to Georgian Bay, a fall of 60 feet. In 1906 a petition was presented to the Canadian Parliament, signed by 112 members, in favour of a 20-foot water-way, the intention being to provide a deep channel capable of taking ocean-going ships to and from the Great Lakes. The capital of the Company was then raised to £10,000,000 stock and £20,000,000 in bonds. The time given for the completion of the works was eight years. The Act contains a clause enabling the Government to take possession of the works on arbitration terms. The canal now authorized does not extend further east than St. Anne's. The Company have power to duplicate the Lachine Canal and locks, or to send their traffic through those water-ways which belong to the Canadian Government. The former course would involve enormous cost, and the latter would probably fail to meet the needs of the traffic, which is already congested at that point. The Company will probably have to find some access for the huge traffic which they expect to carry from the lakes to the St. Lawrence other than that through the Lachine locks. The Back River, on the north side of Montreal, may possibly be selected as a convenient access from the Ottawa to the St. Lawrence Rivers.

Two opinions are held as to what the depth of the proposed water-way should be. Some lake traders contend that steamers constructed for lake trade and economical carriage of grain and ore are not suited for ocean trade. They assert, indeed, that the cost of trans-shipment of grain has now been reduced to so low a figure that the owner of a lake grain steamer will find it more economical to discharge his cargo into an elevator or into barges at the entrance to the canal, than to send his steamer down the canal to Montreal or to Quebec for shipment of grain at those ports. These traders are in favour of a shallower canal with longer locks. They state that the cheapest way and the most convenient will be to tow the grain in large barges the full length of the canal. The capital, which would have to be very great for deepening the canal from 12 feet to 28 feet, would, these traders urge, be better expended in the adequate equipment of the canal, the provision of terminal accommodation at each end of it, the construction of an independent entrance to the St. Lawrence, and the provision of barges, tugs, power-houses, and elevators.

Another section, and that probably the larger and the more far-seeing, contend that the vast trade between the Great Lakes and the St. Lawrence cannot be adequately provided for and developed in any other way than by a water-way of at least 20 feet in depth with continuous and un-interrupted access direct from the St. Lawrence to Georgian Bay. The advocates of a ship canal point to the comparatively small traffic passing through the Welland Canal, and to the failure of the Erie Canal as a commercial highway. To the argument that a 20-foot water-way will cost at least £20,000,000, they reply that if the State of New York can afford to spend a similar sum in deepen-ing the Erie Canal only to 14 feet, the Dominion is rich enough to undertake the Georgian Bay enterprise. If such a water-way is built, large steamers will ply between Quebec or Montreal and Chicago, or the other ports on Lake Superior. Special steamers may even be built to trade between the Lake ports and Liverpool, or other European ports.

The Canal Company expect, when the canal is built, to be able to deliver grain from Chicago to Montreal for shipment to Europe at a price of 3 cents per bushel, as compared with $4\frac{1}{2}$ cents at the American ports. Montreal, moreover, is 300 miles nearer to Liverpool than New York. The opening of this navigation would place the Canadian lake fleet, it is contended, on the same advantageous footing as that at present enjoyed by the United States lake fleet. The former would be able to carry from United States western lake ports to Montreal and Quebec, but the latter could not do so from any Canadian lake port. This would insure the carriage of every bushel of Canadian wheat in a Canadian bottom.

The Canal Company, who have expended large sums of money in making elaborate surveys and taking complete soundings, presented their plans to the Government for approval nearly twelve months ago. They have given notice of a Bill now before the Canadian Legislature for further and wider powers. The pivot round which so much in Canadian politics turns, is the problem how to develop the vast natural resources of the Dominion, and to provide adequate means of transportation by rail, road, and water. The Georgian Bay project has come within the range of practical politics, and, if constructed as a deep water-way, it appears to its advocates to be destined to play as important a part in Canadian history as the Panama Canal will in that of American commerce, or the Suez Canal has

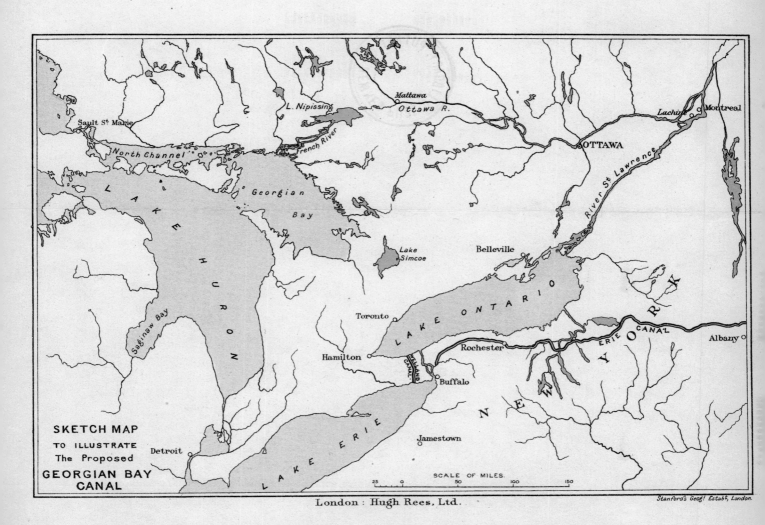

SKETCH MAP

TO ILLUSTRATE

The Proposed

GEORGIAN BAY
CANAL

London : Hugh Rees, Ltd.

Stanford's Geog! Estab^t, London.

SCALE OF MILES.

Sault St Marie

North Channel

L. Nipissing

Mattawa

Ottawa R.

French River

Lachine · Montreal

OTTAWA

River St Lawrence

LAKE HURON

Georgian Bay

Lake Simcoe

Belleville

Saginaw Bay

Toronto

LAKE ONTARIO

Hamilton

Rochester

ERIE CANAL

Albany

WELLAND CANAL

Buffalo

Detroit

LAKE ERIE

Jamestown

NEW YORK

played on the other side of the Atlantic. In short, it is evident that the interest manifested in the formation of artificial water-ways is being felt in America and Canada as in all other civilized countries, and that the vast economical improvement offered by such undertakings is being recognized there.

THE PANAMA CANAL

Towering above all other projects connected with water-ways, the Panama Canal calls wonder from everyone. When this great water-way is finished —and its advocates deny that there is any longer a doubt as to this—not only will the geographical conditions of Southern America be transformed, but the commercial situation all the world over will be altered too.

The great trade route of the world which has flowed for centuries the length of the Mediterranean, from East to West, once made the warehouses and markets of the Levant synonyms of wealth and luxury. The greatness of the Turk, the rise of Venice, the growth of Alexandria, were all fostered and developed by the flow of the golden tide. The Mediterranean, by virtue of the merchant shipping which swept its surface, became the highroad of the world, the strategical centre of naval activity, the scene of the greatest naval actions of past or present times, the spot chosen by the fates for the destinies of Empires were to be decided.

The conditions of the eastern Mediterranean will some day be reproduced in the western Atlantic. The flow of trade from East to West will press

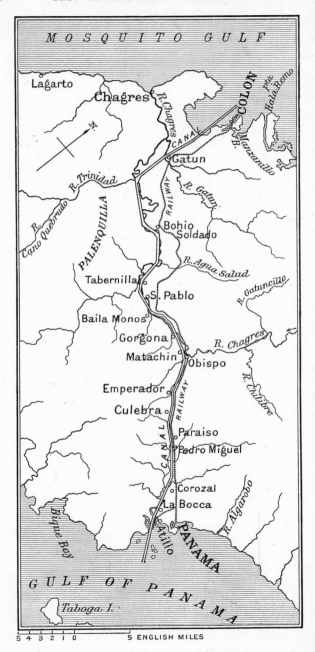

on through the Atlantic to pierce the American continent at its centre. Territories and cities lying in the immediate neighbourhood of the great water-way of the future will draw from it life and vigour, as Constantinople and Venice once drew them from the waters of the Mediterranean. The islands of the Caribbean Sea will quite possibly become the strategical vantage points that Malta and Gibraltar are to-day. Gigantic in its material aspect as is the daring project, it is the possibilities, political and commercial, bound up with it, that baffle most completely our powers of measurement.

As, of course, we all know, the project was origin-ally the offspring of French energy and French intellect. How the French project miscarried and failed we need not here discuss. All we need to record is that it *did* fail, and that the United States stepped into the place of the European Republic and took up the burden that had been laid down.

For years not a little controversy and a good deal of doubt surrounded the question as to the exact spot where the new canal was to be con-structed. But a few years back it was thought that Nicaragua would be the chosen spot. Now, after some controversy, the choice has fallen finally on Panama. The little Republic of Colombia, it is true, made difficulties some years ago, but these have been overcome, and the construction proceeds in Panama.

The choice which fell on that region was not dictated by any prepossessions in favour of it. On the contrary, the experiences of France should have been enough to deter the most daring from proceeding with the work which had already cost many lives. Panama has, in fact, few resources, and an execrable climate. It is a poor country, low-lying, the reverse of fertile, with only some 300,000 inhabitants. But with all these disadvantages the claims of Panama have prevailed, and it is there that the great link between the Atlantic and the Pacific will be cut.

When it assumes concrete shape it will be recognized as a monument to the personal energy and determination of Mr. Roosevelt. It was his courage and determination that scared the Republic of Colombia from pressing their opposition, swept objections aside, and sent them to meet the fate resistance based on sordid grounds usually receives when it encounters such political forces as were wielded by the President.

A description of the construction of this canal in the *Times Engineering Supplement* of May 27, 1908, has supplied the following information, which will be of interest to those to whom the subject appeals.

The greatest rise and fall of the tide on the Atlantic side of the canal is about 2·2 feet, whilst on the Pacific side it is 20 feet. The length of the canal under the present scheme will be forty-nine miles, of which thirty-nine will be through hilly country, involving work of a difficult nature, from Bohio to Pedro Miguel. The maximum depth which has still to be excavated will be 127 feet. This does not take into account the large amount of work already accomplished by the French companies on the old sea-level canal, which, taken roughly, represents the excavation of the canal over thirty-six miles, with a maximum depth of 150 feet. Ships, on entering the canal from the Atlantic side, after steaming up eight miles of dredged water-way, will come to Gatun, where will be situated three sets of twin locks in steps one above the other, each set having a lift of 28·3 feet, or a total rise of 85 feet. Each lock will be 1,000 feet long by 100 feet broad, with a maximum depth of 45 feet of water. After passing the locks the ships will emerge into a vast artificial lake covering some 220 square miles, formed by the erection of the Gatun Dam, which is to be constructed of earth, and whose dimensions are to be: 7,600 feet long on top, 2,630 feet thick at the base, and 135 feet high. The slope on the inside will be 3 to 1, and on the outside 2 to 1 down to water-level, below which it will be 25 to 1. On the present high ground at the centre of the dam there will be a broad weir for the overflow of flood-water, which will discharge into the old Chagres River, thus preventing possible damage to the canal.

It is calculated that the worst floods known in the Chagres Valley, which at times raised the river in places 7 feet to 10 feet above the Panama Railway, will not raise the lake to be created more than 2 feet above the 85-foot level.

Leaving Gatun, ships will proceed through the lake and canal for thirty-one miles, arriving at the twin locks of Pedro Miguel, where they will be dropped down 30 feet to emerge into another artificial lake, steaming through which for six miles will bring them to the Sosa twin locks, which are built in two sets, each set having a drop of 27·5 feet. On emerging from these locks they will be in the dredged channel, and steaming down this for about five miles more, will actually be in the Pacific Ocean at a depth where dredging is unnecessary.

The time for passing a ship through each lock will probably be forty to fifty minutes, and it is estimated that the average time of a vessel passing through the entire forty-nine miles of canal will not exceed twelve hours, and will probably be less. The locks are to be fitted with guard gates and movable dams to provide against accidents, and will be built of concrete; the gates are to be operated by electricity. The dredging is being carried out at both the Pacific and Atlantic entrances by both ladder and " dipper " dredgers, the latter provided with dippers of 5 cubic yards capacity. There still remains 150,000,000 cubic yards of material to be moved, including the filling in of dams and around locks, etc., and it is hoped that the canal, with all locks, will be finished in 1915.

It has been suggested that it will take a long time for the Chagres River to fill up the huge lake behind the Gatun Dam, but it is proposed to allow the lake to form gradually whilst the dam is in course of erection, and to commence to fill it as soon as the dam has attained the height of 20 feet, an overflow being provided so that the water can in no case come within 10 feet of the top of the dam as it is being built. By this procedure it is hoped to have the greater part of the water in the lake by the time the dam is finished. What leakage there may be through the bottom or sides of the lake must be a matter which only the filling of the lake can decide.

The scheme of the big lake, among many advantages, has two prominent features : first, it makes any danger to the canal and structures from flood-water unlikely; secondly, it decreases the time necessary for ships to pass through the water-way by enabling them to steam for some thirty miles through the lake at a much greater speed than is possible in a canal.

NATURAL WATER-WAYS IN THE FAR EAST

In the Far East the influence of water-ways, natural and not artificial, is very marked. The food-supply of Northern China now comes from the valley of the Yangtze. England can send her warships up as far as Nanking—that is to say, 230 miles from the sea—and ships of considerable size as far as Hankow, 400 miles inland. Small vessels even ply as far as Ichang, 600 miles further up the river.

The rivers of Northern Manchuria also influence the question of supply, and, therefore, of strategy too. For example, Harbin is situated on the eastern bank of the Sungari River, some 250 miles, as the crow flies, above its juncture with the Amur, and some 125 miles (measured similarly) downstream from Kirin. It is an important strategical centre, and the middle point of a water route running

10

north and south, which links the first line of Russia's defence and the first line of communication (the Trans-Manchurian Railway) with the second line of defence and the second line of communication (the Amur and the projected Amur railway). This Sungari River, which links the two Pacific coast routes together, is sufficiently deep in spring and summer to carry shallow-draught vessels from the Upper Yangtze by way of Vladivostock to Nicolaievsk, up the Amur and its own waters to Harbin. In other words, it is physically possible to travel 3,000 miles by water from the heart of Central China to the heart of Central Manchuria.

Again, the Sungari has many important tributaries which furnish water communication with very distant points in Central and Northern Manchuria. Chief of these tributaries is the Nonni River, which is actually navigable by small craft 400 miles above the point where it falls into the Sungari. The rivers Hurka and Tung, and a host of lesser streams, can be used by junks or small native boats for dozens of miles in many different directions.

The Sungari and its tributaries, therefore, drain a huge area, and it has been stated[1] that the three million acres of land immediately adjoining them are of the richest description. Vast possibilities are therefore connected with this region. Wheat—the principal crop—and Manchurian flour will in the future supply with food a large proportion of the people of the Eastern world. But Chinese agriculture

---

[1] *Vide The Coming Struggle in Eastern Asia,* by B. L. Putnam Weale.

will not be confined to this region alone; North-Eastern Mongolia will be invaded, and the rich grass country on the east of the Gobi Desert will be brought under cultivation. Eventually a great belt of land, producing wheat, will grow up, and a nation in her need will know how to make use of the supplies it will offer. The railway communications from Harbin are already stretching out their arms over the promised land, and will place them at the disposal of armies—whether Russian or Japanese remains yet to be determined — and that city may in the future have millions of tons of corn at the disposal of her mills. The wheat need not, necessarily, have been grown by Russia, for in any case the Chinese will persistently push forward, and make progress where economical difficulties block the way of emigration and settlement to the European Power.

Siberia, of which much has already been said, possesses in its rivers a means of communication and of agricultural development even superior to what is usually afforded by railways. Its important river system seems to have been created for the purpose of developing the land, and of serving as a system of feeders to any railway system traversing the country from west to east.[1]

The great rivers of Ob and Irtisch, and that still more important stream the Yenisei, rising in water-sheds far to the south of the Trans-Siberian railway, flow in ever-increasing volume towards the north, until at last they fall into the Arctic Ocean some 3,000 miles from their sources. Large

[1] *The Coming Struggle in Eastern Asia,* p. 262.

steamers can navigate the Yenisei for 2,000 miles. The Ob, and its most important tributary the Irtisch, have a carrying power hardly less extensive. Taking these water-ways, their tributaries, and the canal system already constructed, into conjunction with one another, all agricultural Siberia can be reached by steamer from the sea.   It is true that land and water are frost-bound during many months of the year, but, even so, the influence of the rivers in this region is immense.   The Siberian railway has stirred popular imagination, and has carried off the honours, while the rivers that have done so much to supplement it have been forgotten.

CHAPTER VIII

STRATEGICAL RAILWAYS IN PROCESS OF CONSTRUCTION

THE STRATEGICAL RAILWAYS OF THE BALKAN PENINSULA

THE remarkable progress of railway construction in Asiatic Turkey during the last quarter of a century is very noticeable. England was first in the field and the Smyrna–Aidin line was built in 1856 by an English company. Within thirty years three other concessions had been obtained by British firms, two of which subsequently fell into French hands, while the third, from Mersina to Adana, still remains in ours. But up to 1885 there were only 240 miles of railway laid in Asiatic Turkey. The period immediately following the arrival of the German military mission, under General Von der Goltz, to reform the Turkish army, showed a different state of things. German influence ousted ours at Constantinople partly because we had recently occupied Egypt and were unsympathetic towards the Porte. German advisers instructed the Sultan to embark on ambitious railway projects, and the concession hunters found their reward. The only concession, however, granted to Englishmen was that connected with the railway from Haifa to Damascus, and that company went into bankruptcy, the line being constructed afterwards by the Turkish Government itself. We have never allowed our diplomacy to develop the employment of British capital, and the case in point illustrates the usual procedure.

Other nations have stepped in where we have hesitated, and have had no doubts as to what their object was and no misgivings in attempting to attain it.

In an article on "The Strategic Railways of Asiatic Turkey," published in the *Morning Post* of May 25, 1906, the following list of constructed railroads is given :

CONSTRUCTED RAILROADS.

Ownership.	Termini.	Route—Via.	Mileage.
German ...	Haidar Pacha–Eregli (Anatolia Railway to Konia)	Ismid, Biledjik, Eskishehr, Kara Hissar, Akshehr, Konia ...	574
German ...	Eskishehr–Angora ...	Beylik Kenpru ...	266
French ...	Mudania–Broussa ...	—	26
French ...	Smyrna–Afioum Kara Hissar	Kassaba, Alashehr, Gubek, Uchak ...	351
British ...	Smyrna–Dinair ...	Balachik, Seraikevi, Bach Tshesme, Chardak	226
British ...	Mersina–Adana ...	Tarsus	40
French ...	Beyrout–Hamah ...	Damascus, Rayak, Baalbek, Homs ...	225
Turkish ...	Haifa–Damascus ...	Nazareth, Samak, Ain Dakar, Mazarib, Sanamein	144
French ...	Jaffa–Jerusalem ...	Ramleh, Deiraban ...	51
Turkish ...	Damascus–Thabouk ...	Maan, Medarawa ...	502
		Total	2,405

PROJECTED RAILROADS.

Ownership.	Termini.	Route—Via.	Mileage.
German ...	Angora–Kaiseria ...	Kirshehr, Hadji Bektach	246
German ...	Samsoun–Sivas ...	Kavak, Amassia, Tokat	225
?	Trebizond–Bayazid ...	Kop Dagh, Erzerum, Kara Killise... ...	357
?	Erzerum–Van ...	Khinis, Tach Han, Djakin	225
German ...	Sivas–Diabekr ...	Dvrighi, Kharput, Arghana	309
German ...	Eregli – Persian Gulf (Bagdad Railway) ...	Adana, Bagtcheh, Kazanali Killis, Tel Habesh, Harran, Nissibin, Mosul, Tekrit, Bagdad, Kerbela, Nedjef, Basra ...	1,143
French ...	Hamah–Tel Basher ...	Maret el Noman, Aleppo	180
Turkish ...	Thabouk–Mecea ...	El Hejer, Medineh ...	620
		Total	3,305

Thus, more than 2,000 miles of railway have been built in the last twenty years, and the second table shows how important from a strategical point of view are the lines not yet commenced. The Germans have absorbed nearly 1,000 miles of railway already constructed, and are responsible for nearly 2,000 miles of the projected lines. The smallness of the British share is conspicuous.

It is noticeable, too, that most of the Levant lines which are in French hands are practically commercial railways. Those for which the Germans have obtained concessions are, on the other hand, mainly strategical, and they carry with them a Turkish kilometric guarantee. Owing to the insufficiency of the revenue derived from the provinces traversed by the German lines, the various projects have been delayed to wait for new Turkish sources of revenue. These, again, are dependent on international agreements.

Interest in Balkan railway projects temporarily waned till the winter of 1908, when in February the Continental press suddenly bubbled with excitement. Austria-Hungary, it was then announced, had persuaded the Sultan to permit her to carry out surveys towards railway construction in a corner of the Balkan Peninsula which many soldiers, and possibly some statesmen, would have been puzzled to quickly indicate upon a map. The railway, like a celebrated baby, might have been forgiven, for it was a very small one—not a hundred miles in length—running from Uvatz through Novi-Bazar to Mitrovitza ; but there were important diplomatic questions hinging on its existence, and politically it possesses a potential value which calls for a few words.

The Treaty of Berlin, while it established peace in Europe, bequeathed us a legacy of strife in connection with railway building in the Balkan Peninsula, in which capitalists, strategists, and statesmen were to be seen scrambling with one another for advantage, personal or patriotic as the case might be. In 1888 the great line from Vienna to Constantinople was opened, and a year later a branch from it joined Nish with the Ægean at Salonika. Railways in Bosnia and Herzegovina were also constructed by Austria uniting Brod, a frontier town of Sclavonia, on the Save, with Sarajevo, Mostar, and Metkovitz, which last-named town

is close to the shores of the Adriatic, on the river
Narenta. Two lines have subsequently been laid to
the south-west and south-east. Ragusa, Trebinje,
and Zelineka, on the northern shore of the Bocche
di Cattaro, have been reached by the former, and it
is intended,[1] by means of a train ferry at Catene, to
continue this line to Badua, Antivari, and Scutari.
On the other hand, the latter of the two lines just
mentioned reached Uvatz, on the frontier of the
Sanjak of Novi-Bazar, in September, 1906. It is
from Uvatz that the proposed line which made
such a stir last winter is to start. That Austria
would endeavour to obtain Turkey's sanction to
an extension of the line through Novi-Bazar to
Mitrovitza, was not unexpected. It was the
manner in which the announcement of an accomplished fact was made that caused the excitement
above referred to. Its survey will probably be
undertaken at once. The plans will be made for a
normal gauge, though it appears doubtful whether
it will not have to be built for a narrow one corresponding to the 76-centimetre gauge of the Bosnian
railways. For the conversion of these Bosnian railways from the narrow gauge which they at present
possess, to a normal gauge, would mean little less
than their practical reconstruction. Such an
operation would cost several millions sterling—a
financial burden too heavy for the occupied
provinces to bear.

It is, therefore, quite probable that the Novi-
Bazar railway will have to be built for a narrow
gauge, and this would certainly suffice for all local

[1] *Vide* a correspondent in the *Times*, February 20, 1908.

needs. The difference of cost between the normal
and narrow gauge line through the Sanjak would
be approximately £1,200,000. The drawbacks of
the narrow gauge might to some extent be counteracted by laying a third rail between the two tracks
of normal gauge lines from Mitrovitza to Uskub, so
that the Bosnian trains might run through from
the Croatian border to the latter place.[1] But no
expedient will avail to save " through " passengers
from the necessity of changing twice, or goods from
the expense of a double unloading and reloading.
Baron von Aehrenthal's dream of the Mitrovitza–
Bosnia railway as a through route from Central
Europe to the Piræus, Egypt, and India, thus
vanishes into smoke, and his line appears as an
undertaking of little commercial but considerable
political significance.

There were, and are, other schemes for railway
construction in the Balkans, and other Powers
have interests which the railroad may assist. Italy
seeks for a port on the eastern shores of the
Southern Adriatic to counteract the ascendancy
in that sea which the possession since 1815 of
Dalmatia has given Austria, and to gain the
strategical advantage which access to the western
flank of the Balkan States will give her. She proposes to build a line of railway into Montenegro,
and on by Mitrovitza to Nish, if practicable. She
has, indeed, acquired Antivari on the Montenegrin
shore, and the project—not a promising one,
however—of converting it into a sea-port has been

[1] *Vide* telegram from the *Times* correspondent in Vienna, dated
May 12, 1908.

set on foot. It is said, indeed, at the time of writing to be finally abandoned, as the Treaty of Berlin conferred on Austria-Hungary the right of maritime and sanitary police over that port, a control which would not render it attractive as the terminus of a Danube–Adriatic railway. Likewise, there has been a revival of the scheme that Moscow might be united with the Adriatic by a direct line of rail running through Rumania, Servia, Northern Albania, and Montenegro. Such a line would strengthen the influence of Russia in the western Balkans, and Servia would welcome the prospect of an outlet for her agricultural produce and live stock on the Adriatic. The proposed line, according to a correspondent of the *Times*,[1] will be united with the Rumanian and Russian systems by a bridge thrown over the Danube at Kladovo or Radmivatz; it will follow the Timok Valley to Nish, probably proceeding thence via Prishtina and Scutari to San Giovanni di Medua,[2] a little south of Antivari on the Adriatic coast. The line in the latter part of its course will follow the valleys of the White and Black Drin. A branch from Scutari to Dulcigno and Antivari is also proposed.

Again, a *Times* correspondent, writing from Vienna under date May 12, 1908, reports a distinct decrease of friction between the Powers interested in the various railway routes. Austria-Hungary and Germany are stated to have given diplomatic sanction to the Servian application for a Turkish

---

[1] Writing from Sofia, February 20, 1908.

[2] *Vide* also information from their own correspondent at Paris, published in the *Times* of June 9 and June 12, 1908.

concession to survey the Merdare-Stimlia section of the projected Danube–Adriatic line. Merdare is the point at which the Trans-Balkan line would pass from Servian into Turkish territory, and Stimlia would be the point where the line would unite with the existing Mitrovitza–Uskub–Salonika railway. The Servian application is understood to be supported by Russia, Italy, and France, and it is expected that it will be granted by the Porte in a short time. The survey, and even the construction of the Mitrovitza–Stimlia section would not prejudice the further question of the route to be followed by the Trans-Balkan line between Stimlia and the Adriatic. Hence, possibly, the willingness of Austria-Hungary and Germany to support the Servian application. The *Times* correspondent at Paris, writing on May 22, 1908, says that a telegram from Rome notifies the early arrival in Paris from that city of the document accepting the financial agreement between the Powers interested in the plan for a Danube–Adriatic railway. France, it is stated, will contribute 45,000,000 francs (£1,800,000) towards the construction of the line, Italy 40,000,000 francs (£1,600,000), and Bulgaria 15,000,000 francs (£600,000).[1]

But there is more to be said. Greece would wish for the Sultan's permission to join the Turkish and Greek railways at Larissa. Such a junction would unite Athens with Europe by rail. An article in the *Saturday Review*, dated February 22,

[1] It is a noticeable fact, which has caused surprise at home and abroad, that Great Britain contributes nothing to the scheme. It seems doubtful, however, whether financial co-operation was desired by us.

1908, supports the claim of Baron von Aehrenthal that the shortest route from Central Europe to the East would then be via Vienna, Pesth, Serajevo, and Athens. The shortest route will eventually command the traffic. It is possible that the route to Egypt and India via Brindisi may some day become subordinate to a new one via Athens. On the other hand, it is contended that the existing connection via Belgrade and Nish will be the shortest, and that there is no necessary connection between the Greek and Austrian railway projects. Meanwhile, a line is being built by an English and French railway company, acting in concert, from the Piræus to the Turkish frontier, and an effort to obtain the Sultan's consent to its extension to Salonika or to some point to the north of Salonika is being made. Should this extension be effected, Athens will be placed in direct communication with Central Europe independently of any other railway which may be constructed.

Thus, concessions for railway construction in an electrical atmosphere such as that of the Balkan Peninsula are jealously scrutinized, and their ultimate effects closely scanned. Commercial and strategical values need to be weighed. The contemplated railway through Novi - Bazar would almost certainly be a financial failure. The branch line which Turkey possesses now from Uskub to Mitrovitza is insolvent, but it has an important strategical value in that it enables Turkey to concentrate an army at the latter place, which would be in a position to act either against Servia or Montenegro and to prevent these Slav states uniting their forces. It also enables Turkey to rapidly meet an Austrian advance eastwards through the passes of the unoccupied Sanjak. Austria would neutralize this advantage by the extension of the line through the Sanjak to Uvatz, thus placing her on an equal footing with her potential enemy.

The proposal to connect the Danube with the Adriatic by railway has, on the other hand, less strategical importance, but gives promise of greater commercial benefit. The new party in Turkey, not fearing Servian aggression, will probably view it more favourably than the other scheme. The " Slav line " would penetrate the heart of Albania, and would link the inland districts of the country with the sea; Albania would thus be opened up, and this outlying province would be brought into closer touch with the remainder of European Turkey.

THE BAGHDAD RAILWAY

What is known as the Baghdad Railway was much discussed some years ago, and widely different views have been hotly urged with regard to it. Mr. Valentine Chirol, in his excellent work[1] on *The Middle Eastern Question*, spoke quite clearly on the subject in 1903, but since then, except when the German press reopened the matter two and a half years ago, it has been shrouded to a great extent in diplomatic mystery, which, for obvious reasons, it would be undesirable for

[1] *The Middle Eastern Question*, by Valentine Chirol. London, John Murray, 1903.

an officer to attempt to dispel. Yet certain facts
of public notoriety may be recorded to exhibit the
state of affairs to-day.

Briefly put, the scheme represents an attempt

RAILWAYS IN ASIATIC TURKEY

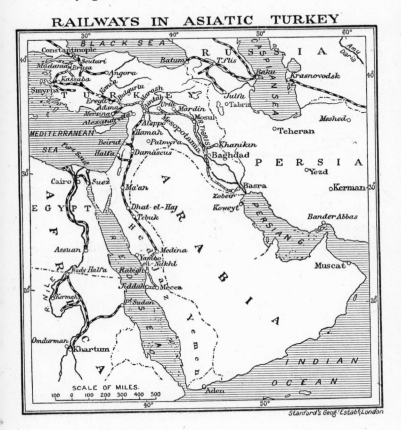

to link together by rail the eastern base of the
Mediterranean with the Persian Gulf. The total
length of the railway may be roughly estimated
at 1,750 miles, and if we add 625 miles for the
existing Anatolian railway, and 400 miles for the

Smyrna–Kassaba and Mersina–Adana railways, which have already passed under German control, the entire system will amount to an aggregate of nearly 2,800 miles, independent of further extensions or the ultimate absorption of the Syrian and Arabian railways. The line is to traverse Asia Minor and Mesopotamia, running from Scutari on the Bosphorus, south-eastwards through Konia, to Adana. Thence it will bend north-westwards to Marash, and then, turning sharply, will once more head south-eastwards to Aintab. From that town it will stretch away eastwards to Urfa, and on to Mardin and Mosul, or ancient Nineveh, from whence the valley of the Tigris will be followed generally to Baghdad. At that city it will strike across from Tigris to Euphrates, and follow the course of the latter, via Basra, very probably, to Koweyt, where it will find a terminus on the Persian Gulf. But as yet it has only got as far as Eregli—more than half-way between Konia and Adana—and before Koweyt or any other port on the Persian Gulf is its terminus there are many difficulties to be overcome—many interests, financial, political, and strategical, to be reconciled. That we are deeply interested, a glance at an atlas will show. The connection of the Hedjaz railway with the Anatolian portion of this line, which will be referred to subsequently, will affect the security of the Egyptian frontier. Koweyt is a port held under British protection, and our interests in the Persian Gulf are such that for a hundred years we have in pure disinterestedness preserved peace and equity over its waters, while the best strategical authorities have declared it a principle[1] of our policy that we shall be predominant in them. Neither of the great parties in the Houses of Parliament have shown any disposition to waver as regards this latter point, and quite recently, when the Anglo-Russian Convention was under discussion, Sir Edward Grey made it clear that he had no intention of departing from the policy his immediate predecessor in office had set up.

The railway is undoubtedly the product of German diplomacy. It has, indeed, been styled "the German railway invasion of Asiatic Turkey." Planned and financed by Germans as it has been, it is not to be supposed that its construction is intended to further interests which are not German. It is true that Germany has been, and is, desirous that both French and English money as well as her own should be put into the undertaking; but that was to secure a surer footing for her diplomacy rather than to benefit financiers of London or Paris. It is political, under the guise of financial, co-operation that Germany is looking for, and therefore our partnership is more valuable to her than that of anyone else. Fears have been expressed in certain quarters that the proposed railway may destroy the existing Bosphorus and Smyrna railway, in which this country is interested, and our Government was urged to discountenance it, and especially its extension to Koweyt.

The various considerations that present themselves to us are as follows: The Baghdad railway

---

[1] Especially interesting in this connection is an article by Captain Mahan in the *National Review* of September, 1902.

will undoubtedly be the shortest route to India. It may, therefore—but this is not so certain as some assume—be the best route for the Indian mails, and, if it proves so, it will be to our interest to use our good offices to provide a proper terminus for it at or near Koweyt. It would manifestly be undesirable that such a railway should be in the hands of foreign to the exclusion of British capitalists. A route such as this would, moreover, provide another opening for trade in the Persian Gulf, therefore it is desirable that it should touch that Gulf within the territories of a Sheik over whom we have extended our protection and with whom we have special treaties. Again, as this railway will traverse a very rich country, it is not irrational to expect that in course of time it will add to the wealth of Turkey, and by so doing will indirectly increase the riches of any other country which is ready to take advantage of Turkey's welfare. At the same time, we have to remember that the political control of vast regions in Asia Minor and Mesopotamia is bound up with the construction of the line, and the establishment of such control in such a locality calls for most vigorous examination.

In 1903 our public men gave us their views on this much discussed matter. Mr. Balfour, speaking in the House of Commons, on the railway, on April 8, 1903, said : " Whether the British producer will be able to take advantage of it is not for me to say ; but the House will have to calculate whether it is desirable that this railway should be constructed with French and German capital, and whether it will be prudent to leave the passenger traffic in the hands of those two nations with whom we are on the most friendly terms, but whose interests are not identical with our own." He further pointed out that if it were better that this great national highway were in the hands of three great countries rather than in those of one or two, and if it were to be in European hands, there was much to be said for it being in the hands partly of this country as well as partly in the hands of France and Germany. But he admitted that the question was full of difficulties, and stated that the Government intended to give the whole subject their most careful consideration. He would not say anything more precise or definite at that time.

On the same day, in reply to Mr. Gibson Bowles, Mr. Balfour said : " There have been no formal communications between His Majesty's Government and any foreign Government on the subject of the Baghdad railway. The proposed railway is not to be a German railway. The subject was referred to in two brief conversations, one with the French and one with the German Ambassador, about thirteen months ago Lord Lansdowne then stated that ' we should not regard the undertaking with unfriendly eyes provided that British capital and British interests were placed at least on terms of equality with those of any other Power.' I am not aware that these conversations have had any results, or have exercised any influence on subsequent events. Communications have been, and are still, going on with British capitalists on the subject. No final arrangements have been arrived at. The proposals under consideration involve no guarantee of a postal or any other subsidy. The suggestions to be made to us are, we understand, (1) that British capital and British control are to be on an absolute equality with the capital and control of any other Power ; (2) that in respect to the negotiations which are now going on with the Turkish Government for a new commercial treaty (and which—quite apart from the Baghdad railway—raise the question of increasing the Turkish Customs), His Majesty's Government should not object to a reasonable increase in these duties, although a part of the increase is to be used in guaranteeing a railway so important for the commercial interests of Turkey ; (3) that, if the railway should prove to be a substantially better route for conveying the mails to India, it may be used for conveying those mails, on terms to be agreed upon hereafter ; (4) that His Majesty's Government should assist, not by money or the promise of money, but by their good offices in providing a proper terminus at or near Koweyt."

Since then Mr. Chirol has written his book, and quite lately the project has again come under public notice. The *Times* correspondent in Berlin, writing on May 21, 1908, says : " The *Frankfurter Zeitung* learns from Constantinople that the Turkish Council of Ministers has unanimously decided to recommend to the Sultan the construction of four additional sections of the Baghdad railway, which would advance the line a distance of 800 kilometres. It is believed that the necessary Irade will shortly be issued, and that the work will be begun without further delay. This extension would include the Taurus section of the line, which has always been described as presenting greater difficulties than any other section. The chief town along the projected track of the railway is Mardin, which lies at a distance of about 800 kilometres from Eregli, the present terminus, and is an important centre some 200 kilometres north-west of Mosul. It is believed that from this point onwards the difficulties which will have to be surmounted in the plains of the Tigris and the Euphrates will prove less considerable." Writing again, from Constantinople, on May 20, 1908, the correspondent of the same paper says : " As the results of the efforts, during the past six weeks, of the Anatolian Railway Company, supported by German diplomacy, the objection of the Porte to mortgaging the surplus of the old ceded revenues of the Ottoman public debt towards guaranteeing further sections of the Baghdad railway has been overcome, and the Council of Ministers on Sunday addressed a Mazbata to the Imperial Chancellory recommending the building of four sections, namely, from Bulgurlu to Helif junction, the station for Mardin, a total length of 840 kilometres, and the pledging of the above-mentioned surplus from the year 1913 for the purpose of the kilometric guarantee. The imperial sanction to the Mazbata will doubtless follow when the Anatolian Railway Company will sign the necessary conventions with the Porte."

Turkey, no doubt, by the raising of the Customs duties—to which consent was given last year—will divert to this line the surplus not required for the payment of debt, and this will be an excellent security for Germany. But in the event of trouble with Turkey, if Germany were one of several Powers interested, her position would be far stronger than though she were alone. Her chief control and the lion's share of advantage must always remain with her, but for Germany to assert herself against Turkey without having a European combination behind her would be a difficult matter. An attempt will probably, therefore, be made to attract British capital towards the line in which British interests are certainly not predominant. It is very doubtful whether British investors will look with any favour on it. We will, no doubt, benefit by all improvements in communications which develop commerce, even though the original object of the communications was certainly not to benefit us. Therefore, while we need not oppose this scheme, we may safely leave British investors to find out whether it is to their interests or not to give it financial support, and we may be fairly certain that our Government will not depart from the custom of former Governments in refusing to make any investment in it on behalf of the State.

The section of the line which has the greatest interest for us will be the last section, because that will terminate with the port, which will form the terminus in the Persian Gulf. It is certain that we shall have to insist on that port being either under British control or distinctly independent. As such independence is not probably attainable in the region in question, the other alternative is the one we shall have to choose.

In this connection a statement of views in the House of Commons on June 16, 1908, by Sir Edward Grey is of interest.   He was asked by Sir E. Sassoon whether he would state to the House the name of the terminus of the Baghdad railway stipulated for by the German Turkish Convention. He replied that "the alignment of the railway is described in Article 1 of the Baghdad Railway Convention of March 5, 1903, which has been published. The terminus of the railway is to be Basra, but a branch line is, according to the Convention, to be built from Zobeir to a point on the Persian Gulf to be hereafter determined."   He was asked by Mr. Ashley whether this point is to be definitely under British influence in the Persian Gulf.   Sir E. Grey stated that he had quoted the original terms of the Convention.   Asked by Major Anstruther Gray whether the British Government will have no voice in the determination as to the terminus, Sir E. Grey stated that the British Government were not concerned in the original railway convention.   Asked by Mr. Rees whether it was contemplated to end the line at Basra, Sir E. Grey answered that he could not say.   He only knew the actual terms of the Baghdad Convention of 1903.   Asked again, by Mr. Smeaton, whether the British Government consented that a railway station should be established at Basra, Sir E. Grey stated that we did not give our consent.   When invited to state his opinion as to any disturbance of the balance of power in the Persian Gulf in consequence of this Convention, Sir E. Grey deprecated raising such wide questions, and stated that the railway was a long way from being carried through.

Thus, as matters now stand, it seems clear enough, viewed from the commercial standpoint, that the railway may be injurious to British undertakings ; while its strategical influence will be even more inimical to our interests in the Middle East. Nevertheless, it is not possible for this country to oppose the construction of the line.   It will satisfy a need which has been felt for many years, and a demand for it exists on commercial grounds alone which it is not possible to gainsay.

THE DAMASCUS—HEDJAZ RAILWAY

In view of what has been said previously as to the Sinaitic Peninsula, the construction of the Hedjaz railway has for us a strong strategical interest.   To Mohammedans generally it appeals, however, chiefly through the force of sentiment, because it is intended to provide an easy path by which the followers of the Sultan may pay that visit to Mecca which every devout Mussulman desires to make, without undergoing the risks and hardships of the long pilgrimage which has hitherto proved to many an unrealized dream.   To us, again, it supplies another illustration of a modern line of communication traversing once more the path by which invaders, centuries ago, led on their followers to victory and occupation.   For it is by the pilgrim route which this railway is to traverse that the earliest Khalifs, moving in a reverse direction, penetrated into Syria.

The present Sultan has thrown himself into the scheme with all the prestige that attaches to his office. He is president of the Hedjaz Railway Commission, and it is certain that its completion will enhance his reputation throughout the Mohammedan world, and will render the task of governing his widely-spread subjects not only physically, but morally easier. Great as is the interest—political, historical, and religious—which this example of latent Turkish energy will rouse, to us it appeals as a most important strategical factor imported into a region where the situation is already one to be watched with vigilance.

Running from Damascus on the eastern side of Jordan, south-westward down the length of Palestine, the railway follows generally the Haj or pilgrims' route to Ma'an. Thence it bends south-eastwards over a bare plateau, waterless and without vegetation, climbs over and sidles down inhospitable rocky mountains to Dhat-el-Haj, and from thence by an arid valley reaches Tebuk. Following the same general direction, it is continued to Medina, having reached that city on September 5, 1908.

At its other extremity it will, in due time, become connected with the Anatolian railway through the railway system of Syria and the continuation of the Baghdad line to Aleppo. The line is narrow gauge, while the lines constructed or being built under German auspices are broad. It is intended, however, that a third rail between the others will obviate break of gauge. The main line is to be linked with Haifa in the Bay of Acre as well as with Beirut; and at the former place a

German syndicate is constructing harbour works
with a view of here establishing a commercial port
on the Syrian coast.   The Port of Alexandretta, also
must ultimately grow greatly in importance when
an outlet is sought for the varied produce supplied
by the rich provinces traversed by the railway lines
with which it is proposed to put that port in connection.   Finally, when the railway communications
are complete, it will be possible for Turkish troops
from Europe, Asia Minor, and Syria to be conveyed
in a few days into the Arabian Peninsula, and
forces may be concentrated on the frontier of Egypt
without a sea voyage or weary marches over waterless sands being undertaken.   On the one hand,
the Sultan will be enabled to tighten his grip
over the unruly Arab tribes whose inaccessibility
is now their strength; on the other, should a
Turkish Sultan ever venture to threaten our security
there, the situation on the northern frontier of
Egypt will become more difficult for us.   Already,
unconnected as it still is with the Anatolian line,
the Hedjaz railway has been usefully employed
in carrying troops to fight the rebels in Yemen,
and in bringing the influence of Constantinople
to bear on the Bedouin tribes.   It has been pointed
out that, as the railway approaches the Holy Cities,
these tribes, who, if not friendly, have hitherto done
little or nothing to interfere with the work, may
grow uneasy at the project of interference with
their vested interests.   For the tribes between
Medina and Mecca live on the pilgrims, and reap
an annual harvest in hiring camels to transport
them from one to the other city.   Many magnates,

too, in these holy places, are interested in this traffic. The pilgrim is, in fact, exploited in Arabia as is the tourist in many a place nearer home. He has, moreover, to face something beyond inconveniences and extortionate prices. Cholera sometimes is a scourge to the caravans, and many thousands perish in the trying journey during such an outbreak as occurred this year. The roads between Mecca and Medina, and the latter city and Yambo-en-Nakhl, are usually infested with Bedouin robbers, extremes of heat and cold are experienced on the high desert, and altogether the pilgrim has to face considerable risks of various kinds when he sets out on his pious journey. It is said that the railway accommodation on such portions of the line as have already been finished is not calculated to greatly lessen hardship. Open trucks afford neither warmth at night nor protection against the sun by day, while supplies are by no means plentiful. But the railway is still in only a half-developed stage, and better sanitary arrangements will, in future, it is hoped, grapple with disease more effectually than was possible last winter (*vide* letter from the *Times* correspondent at Cairo, dated April 25, 1908).

Yet we may feel sure that a work which fires the imagination of Mohammedans, is carried on under such powerful auspices, and is intended to meet a keenly felt demand, will eventually be completed. The birthplace of Christianity and Islam will then be linked together. The widely separated places which two great religions regard as the holiest on earth will be brought, as it were, within touch of one another. All who are capable of being moved by religious sentiment or the romance of history cannot but be impressed by such a development in the communications of the world. But to soldiers the railway will appeal on quite other grounds, and sentiment will be forgotten when its strategical importance is reviewed. What devotees and philosophers will welcome with the gratitude of a benign expectation, our officers will receive, if not with anxiety, at any rate without satisfaction. While the former may rejoice that pious pilgrims will find it easier to fulfil their religious duty, the latter will, at the same time, look askance at a work which may render it easier for other than pilgrims to do what may some day be regarded as their duty also.

THE AMUR RAILWAY

The late war and its consequences, the risks run and since revealed, have roused anxiety in Russian officials, and made them doubt as to whether the railway across Northern Manchuria can any longer be regarded as trustworthy—that is to say, trustworthy as a means of communication during another great war. Such railways are at all times open to the enterprising raider, but this one is especially so, because much of the territory through which it runs will more probably be colonized by Chinamen than by Europeans, and it cannot, therefore, be safeguarded by the settlement of Russian immigrants along its length—whether for colonizing purposes or with a view to future operations, we need not stay to inquire.   Where Russia is concerned, the purposes of her railways are always twofold, and represent both strategical and commercial policies.   A second line in a more secure position to supplement the one already in existence would clearly be of advantage, and in certain eventualities might become a necessity.   The construction of a railway along the line of the Amur is, indeed, only one more illustration of the indomitable persistency and steadfastness of purpose of Russian policy, for the idea of such a line along the left bank of that river, is no new thing.   It began to be considered as long ago as 1896.   It was then, for certain reasons, abandoned in favour of the more direct Manchurian line, but it has once more been taken up, when Russia is once more collecting herself together after the shaking she received in her last great struggle.

In the spring of 1907 the Emperor gave his authority for the construction of the first section of the new line from Nerchinsk, on the Trans-Baikal railway, to Povrovka, the junction of the rivers Shilka and Amur.   The Duma, however, asserted its newly-found power and declined to sanction the enterprise.   In consequence, but little progress beyond some spade-work was accomplished.   The erection of rest-houses at Nerchinsk, some surveying, the establishment of telegraph and telephonic communications for 100 miles, and steps taken towards the purchase of rails, were, however, some instalments towards the great project that were carried through.

The present proposal, which passed the Duma and Council of Ministers in May, 1908 (though not without evoking some opposition), is to construct a line from Kuenga, south-west of Stretensk, on the Trans-Baikal railway, up the valley of the river Kuenga, across the watershed of the rivers Kuenga and Nerch, and into the valley of the river Urgum. The line will then cross the watershed into the valley of the Amazar and continue east, with the river Amur on the right, and the Stanovoi Range and rivers Ur and Zeya on the left. It is then intended to carry it over the Zeya near the village of Vvedenovka, from which point the most thickly populated and, in an agricultural sense, the most promising of the districts of the Amur territory will be traversed. The river Bureya and the Lagar-Aul Range are the next obstacles to be overcome, and the line will then follow the valley of the Great Bira to Khabarovsk. The length of the railway from Kuenga to Khabarovsk will be about 1,230 miles, or, including the branch along the river Zeya to Blagovyeshchensk, 1,330 miles. The line is to be of single track, prepared for doubling if necessary. It is to be built by cheap and easy stages in two main sections. The western section, Kuenga to the river Zeya, to be completed in 1911, the eastern section, river Zeya to Khabarovsk, in 1912.

Permission has been given for the construction of the first section of 122 miles from the starting-point at Kuenga, for commencement of work on the Zeya-Khabarovsk section, for expenditure on general survey work, for making a topographical map for a width of 83 miles along the Amur from its junction with the Tungu to the point where the eastern section of the line will cross the river Bureya, and for ascertaining the best method of taking the line across the rivers Bureya and Amur. The bridge across the Amur will be a formidable undertaking, and its construction will demand much time.

Official estimates place the cost of construction at £22,500,000, but hostile critics contend that the total outlay, including money spent on building forts for the protection of the line, will probably amount to £60,000,000.

The project has met with adverse criticism from Liberals, who contend that money should not be assigned to the uninhabited confines of the Empire which is urgently required at home, not only for educational purposes and the promotion of agriculture, but for much-needed reorganization, and strengthening of army and navy, and the defence of other frontiers.

It is also contended that the construction of the line is strategically unsound, that it will be impossible to defend it in war, that the Russian forces in Trans-Baikal and in the littoral province will be separated, and that Vladivostock will become a second Port Arthur.

The Minister of Finance has stated that the country can well afford the cost of the Amur line and other collateral expenses spread over six or more years, and the Government has declared that only one section of the line will now be constructed, after which the Duma will again be consulted.

THE NORTHERN NIGERIAN RAILWAY

In August, 1907, our Government introduced,
and very quickly passed, a Bill for the construction

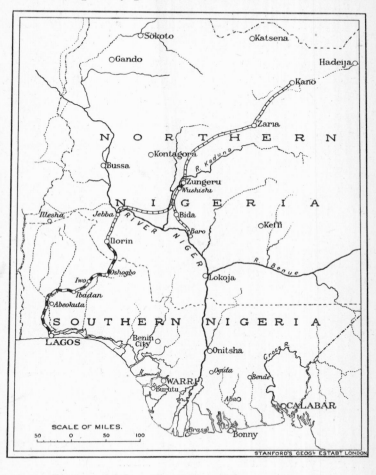

of a railway which will add another means of communication to our scattered Empire, and will be of
supreme commercial benefit to the inhabitants of

Northern Nigeria. Though commercial rather than strategical, it will have a strategical influence, and is therefore dealt with in this chapter. This line is to start from Baro, 70 miles up the Niger, at the head of its navigable portion, and is to run to Kano, the capital of Hausaland, some 500 miles away to the north. It is expected that the line will reach Zungeru at the end of 1909, Zaria in 1910, and Kano a year later.

Northern Nigeria has grown with an ease and rapidity most satisfactory. It was only in January, 1900, that we made our first definite efforts, and took over a small portion of the country. Already we control a vast region dotted with populous towns, and do so with little apparent effort and with but small exercise of armed force. Five years ago a few British soldiers and a weak force of auxiliaries seized Kano and Sokoto, and so firmly established our authority that a large and by no means uncivilized population are placing themselves under our protection, and appear likely to willingly accept our permanent rule. Obviously the railway, in opening good communication through the country, will be of immense assistance to us both in a military and administrative sense. It is to cost about £1,250,000 ; but that is a small price for it even if viewed only as a commercial undertaking. Lancashire wants a freer flowing supply of raw cotton, and cotton is a crop which is steadily increasing in Nigeria, and will, we may hope, continue to do so. None of the countries from which we have any expectation of drawing this valuable raw material in future appear to possess equally

12

good facilities for its production ; and the strides
made during the last four years are not only a
practical demonstration of what has been done, but
a very solid basis of promise of what we may expect.
" The leaps and bounds " of Mr. Gladstone's rhetoric
in another connection are not out of place here.   At
Lagos the crop in 1903 gave us 500 bales,[1] which in
the next year increased to 2,000, and in the next
three years improved to 3,200, 6,000, and 12,000
bales respectively.   In quoting these figures we are
measuring the supply of Lagos alone.[2]   When
cotton plantations are spread over the whole of
Northern Nigeria we shall have some reason for
disappointment if the rate of increase is not
enormously greater.   And as it develops a demand
for transport will in due course bring about further
subsidiary railways ; these in turn will create communities and settlements of a civilized character
along their length.   The status of the inhabitants
will be raised, new needs will arise, and will have
to be satisfied.   In a word, the old tale will be
repeated, crops will call for communications, and
these will bring commerce and civilization.

But the main interest to soldiers is the strategical
advance, which keeps pace with and renders possible
the development of cultivation.   Northern Nigeria
is broken up amongst a number of petty chieftains,
prone to break out into rebellion, and resenting the
restraining influence of our predominance.   To
deal with such opponents good communications
have always been the first necessity of strategy.
The railway will as steadily and surely wear down

---

[1] *Vide* the *Times*, August 23, 1907.   [2] *Ibid*.

whatever remains of turbulence and slave-raiding in Nigeria as it has done in the Sudan ; and with tranquillity firmly established, the process by which communications and commerce grow will once more be repeated.   Northern Nigeria and its railways may appeal to future generations as a good investment when the strategists and soldiers who gained it for them are forgotten.

CHAPTER IX

PERSIA

PERSIA measures 1,450 miles from north-west to south-east, while the shortest distance, from the head of the Persian Gulf to the Caspian, is only 450 miles. Its area comprises 628,000 square miles, but of these a very considerable proportion is desert.

Bounded on the north by the Trans-Caucasus, the Caspian, and the Russian Trans-Caspian region, on the west by Turkish Armenia, Kurdistan, and Mesopotamia, on the south-west and south by the Persian Gulf and Gulf of Oman, it marches on the east with Baluchistan, and Afghanistan, till, in the neighbourhood of the Sarakhs, it again touches a Russian frontier in Turkistan, and trends north-westward with it, till it again strikes the Caspian to the north of Astrabad. The southern shore of that sea practically forms the boundary till Russian territory is again met with at Astara.

Speaking generally, the area thus enclosed is an arid plateau, having an average altitude of from 4,000 to 8,000 feet, with a strip of maritime plain lying below the escarpment on the north and south. Near the north, west, and south-west margin lofty mountain ranges are found running generally north-west and south-east.   In the province of Azerbijan, west of the Caspian, the principal ranges are the Kara Dagh, lying east and west on the south side of the river Aras, and constituting a formidable obstacle.   The Talish Mountains fringe the western shores of the Caspian.   In this northern corner, too, tower Mount Ararat (17,000 feet), Savalan (15,800 feet), Sahend (11,800 feet), and other peaks. These masses are continued eastwards along the northern edge of the plateau by the huge Elburz Mountains, of which Demavend (19,400 feet) is the highest point.   Striking off from the south-eastern corner of the Caspian the Kopet Dagh range shuts in Persia from the Trans-Caspian region.   Further south, and parallel to that range, stretch the Ala Dagh and Binalud Kuh Mountains, and behind them, again, rise the Jagatai Mountains and other minor ranges of rugged hills.   These ranges, stony and sterile, with deep gorges between them, average from 9,000 to 11,000 feet in height.   In the district of Birjand a series of mountains rise sharply from the plains to heights of from 7,000 to 11,000 feet.   Facing the Gulf of Oman, other less lofty ranges, parallel to one another, run from east to west, and form the southern escarpment of the great plateau.

There are no rivers in Persia which are navigable except the Karun, which flows from Shuster into the Shat-el-Arab (confluence of the Euphrates and Tigris), at the head of the Persian Gulf.   Steamers belonging to Messrs. Lynch and Co., who have done much to develop our seaborne trade with

Persia, run from Mohammerah to the Ahwaz Rapids, above which small steamers can ply as far as Shuster by both branches of the river.

The climate varies widely in the different provinces of the country, but over the whole of the plateau the heat in summer and the cold in winter are excessive. The air, however, is dry, and the country in consequence, except in the low-lying parts, may be regarded as healthy. The rainfall is very small, and there is none at all during the summer months. In the mountainous parts of the west there is much snow in winter. Irrigation is largely resorted to during the hot months, when without it little or no cultivation could be accomplished.

Sheep's and goats' wool and lambskins, of which the best come from Khorasan, are important natural products. There is a considerable trade in silk and silk stuffs, produced chiefly in Khorasan and the Caspian Provinces, and in shawls and carpets. Large quantities of cotton, wheat, barley and rice, drugs and gums, are likewise produced. Fruit is plentiful throughout the country. Opium is also largely cultivated, and its export is increasing. Great quantities of minerals exist. The development of all resources, however, is much retarded owing to the want of good roads and the great distances to shipping ports or markets that have be to traversed.

The principal centres of commerce are Tabriz, Teheran, and Isfahan, while the chief ports are found at Bandar Abbas, Linga, and Bushire on the Persian Gulf, and Astara, Enzeli, Meshed-i-Sar (the port of Barfrush), Mahmudabad (the port of Amol), and Bender-i-Gez, in Astrabad Bay, on the Caspian.

The shores of the Persian Gulf are low and sandy, forming a border from 15 to 20 miles wide between the sea and the plateau. The land here is mostly barren, the climate moist, the heat intense and trying. Fevers and malaria are prevalent, and the region generally is unhealthy. The lower basin of the Karun is, however, very fertile ; mules and horses are bred, and sheep and goats yield a plentiful supply of wool. Forty miles from the coast, up the Shat-el-Arab, is situated Mohammerah, a recently developed port and important trading centre.

The most striking feature of Persian geography lies in the two immense deserts which shut off Khorasan from the rest of Persia on the west and south. These are known as Dasht-i-Kavir, or Great Salt Desert, and Dasht-i-Lut, or Great Sand Desert, which lies to the south of the other. Together they stretch from north-west to south-east for more than 650 miles. Their general elevation is not more than 2,000 feet.

Between these deserts and the mountainous regions to the west are situated the plateau provinces of Persia—Teheran, Irak-ajemi, Isfahan, Fars, and Luristan. To the east of Isfahan lies Yezd, and south-west of the Dasht-i-Lut is situated Kerman. These provinces are throughout of a hilly nature, and mountainous in the north, north-west, and south-east, where altitudes as great as 8,500 feet are reached. In Kerman the limestone mountains are said to be as high as 15,000 feet. The fertility of the soil varies directly with the water-supply. Yezd is sandy and barren, so, too, is the greater part of Luristan, and parts of Isfahan are of the same character. Apart from orchards and thorny scrub, this region of plateau is almost destitute of trees.

There are no important rivers ; the Zendeh flowing past Isfahan into the brackish swamp termed Lake Gavekhoneh, the Kur flowing into Lake Niriz, of similar character, and the Kara-Chai flowing into a newly formed lake, Hauz-i-Sultan, between Teheran and Kum, are the most important. Lake Urumiah, in the extreme north-west, is 80 miles long, and from 20 to 30 miles wide.

The chief town of the country, and its capital, is Teheran (280,000 inhabitants). Other important towns are Barfrush, near the southern shore of the Caspian, of 50,000 inhabitants, and Semnan, Damghan, Shahrud, and Mashad (each of 60,000 inhabitants), east of the capital. North-west of it are Resht and Kazvin (each of from 30,000 to 40,000 inhabitants), Sultanieh, Zinjan, and Tabriz (200,000 inhabitants). On the south are Kum, 30,000 to 40,000 inhabitants (at an altitude of 3,100 feet) ; Kashan (3,707 feet), with from 30,000 to 40,000 inhabitants ; and Isfahan, the former capital (5,200 feet), with 80,000 inhabitants. West of Kum and Kashan are Hamadan (6,280 feet), with 30,000 to 40,000 inhabitants, Nehavend, Burujird, Sultanabad, which is the centre of the carpet industry, and Khunsar. West of Lake Niriz lies the important town of Shiraz, with 50,000 inhabitants ; and on its east Kerman, with 60,000 inhabitants.

Communications in Persia are far from good. As has been said, the rivers are next to none ; so were the carriage roads till 1903, when those from Teheran to Kum and Resht alone existed. Lately, however, good roads have been made from Tabriz to Julfa, on the Russian frontier, Resht to Teheran, Kazvin to Hamadan, Mashad to Askabad, with some others in process of construction. With these exceptions, the principal routes are little more than tracks. In the south two enter the country from Bushire and Bandar Abbas. The former is chiefly used by those going to Teheran, and runs by Shiraz, Isfahan, and Kashan. Some steep passes must be climbed before Shiraz is reached, while on the plateau passes as high as 9,000 feet above the sea-level have to be traversed. From Bandar Abbas tracks lead to Kerman (380 miles), Yezd (580 miles), Isfahan (780 miles), and Mashad (950 miles). Shuster and Isfahan are also connected by tracks crossing passes as high above sea-level as 11,000 feet. A route on the west runs from Baghdad, via Kermanshah and Hamadan, to Teheran (410 miles from the frontier). The route, however, now, and always, most in use is that from Trebizond, via Erzerum, Bayazid, Khoi, Tabriz, Kazvin, to Teheran. Another much-frequented route is that connecting Teheran with Mashad, via Semnan, Shahrud, Sabzevar, and Nishapur.

In 1898 Messrs. Lynch and Co. took over a concession granted to a Persian subject for a caravan road between Ahwaz and Isfahan, and sunk considerable capital in improving the road, and in the construction of two bridges of iron and one of stone. This road was opened to traffic in the autumn of 1900. In 1903 the same enterprising firm acquired the concessionary rights of the Imperial Bank of Persia for the roads Teheran–Kum–Isfahan and Kum–Mohammerah, and formed the Persian Road and Transport Company, which started construction on the Kum–Isfahan section in the summer of 1904.

There are practically no railways in the country, the only line being that from Teheran to Shah-Abdul-Azim, about six miles in length. One which traversed the twelve miles from Mahmudabad to Amol, proved an abortive undertaking, and has long been disused.

Messrs. Lynch and Co., it may be noted, are running a steamer once a fortnight up the Karun to Ahwaz, under a subsidy from the British Government.

In consequence of misgovernment the country is in a general state of decay, and even the chief towns are often semi-ruinous. At the moment of writing the political situation is most disturbed, and the outlook uncertain. The army is of Oriental type—ill-organized, ill-trained, and recruited with difficulty. On paper it consists of seventy-nine battalions of infantry, twenty-three batteries of artillery, and a battalion of pioneers. There are also at the capital two so-called Cossack regiments, each 400 strong, and a battery of horse artillery. These troops are organized and trained after Russian models by Russian officers. Some 60,000 regulars

possibly exist, and are probably paid for. Some
50,000 irregular horse, and an uncertain number
of foot soldiers may supplement them.

Such is a brief description of the geographical
features of a country in which we have been for
long much interested. Our anxiety rose mainly
from the desire of Russia to find an outlet to the
Indian Ocean for the same reasons, ostensibly
commercial, which caused her to seek ports on the
Mediterranean and on the Pacific. Now, a harbour
offering such an outlet would be of no use to Russia
unless she could also be mistress of the country
behind it through which her communications lay.
Further, when Russia had established such a seaport
and coaling station she would inevitably wish to
fortify it and the harmless commercial port, like
Batoum in the Black Sea, would soon become a
powerful fortress. The Russian statesman De
Witte, has, in fact, frankly suggested the occupation by Russia of a fortified port on the Persian
Gulf, connected with Russian territory by a railway
which, if not military, would be guarded by troops.

In other words, to gain an outlet on the Indian
Ocean Russia must push her territories down to
the edges of the shore. Accordingly, her policy
for years past has been to gradually assimilate
Persia in the same way as she has assimilated the
Khanates of Central Asia. She wished Persia to
be weak and discontented that she might the more
easily " protect," and perhaps finally annex, her.
In 1890 she entered on an agreement with Persia
by which railway construction in that country was
placed solely in her hands, and ten years ago (1898),

when she became the principal creditor of that country on the security of its customs, her position in Persia was made much stronger.

She has, in fact, if not in name, absorbed the northern portion of Persia already. Mashad has been practically a Russian city for several years.[1] The rich province of Khorasan is to all intents and purposes Russianized. For not very long will the completion of a railway from Askabad to Mashad be delayed, and it has already reached Kettichinar.[2] Enzeli, the port of Resht, was described six years ago by a visitor " as a piece of the foreshore of Nijni Novgorod, or some other town on the Volga," so completely had it become denationalized.[3]

The moment for effective remonstrance has gone by. The thing is there. We cannot hope to free the north of Persia; all we can do is to preserve the remainder of Persia from meeting the same fate which has befallen the north.

For such an absorption of Persia by Russia as has been foreshadowed in the north would affect us in three ways: First, as regards the question of the naval command of the Persian Gulf; secondly, as regards the defence of India ; and, thirdly, as regards the commercial prosperity of India. The naval aspect of the establishment by Russia of a naval base on the Persian coast, flanking our lines of sea communication with India, Australia, and the Far East, has been discussed by various great

---

[1] *Russia in Central Asia*, by Lord Curzon, p. 275.
[2] *Through Biluchistan and Eastern Persia*, by Lord Ronaldshay.
[3] *Pioneer Mail*, September 26, 1902.

authorities, and especially by Captain Mahan, with whom Colonel Mark Bell—whose opinion commands respect—is in agreement.

The control of the Persian Gulf by a foreign State of considerable naval strength, even though we could unquestionably check her naval enterprises, would demand a detachment large enough to affect seriously the strength of our naval strategical position. To secure the natural rights of India, and our communications with her and our possessions further to the east, British naval preponderance in the Persian Gulf must be unfettered, and such a strategical condition is incompatible with the establishment of foreign arsenals on that Gulf. Concessions in the Persian Gulf, whether deliberate or due to neglect of local commercial interests underlying political and military control, "will imperil Great Britain's naval situation in the Far East, her political position in India, her commercial interests in both, and the imperial tie between ourselves and Australasia."[1]   In short, it is admitted by both political parties that we cannot tolerate any interference with our naval supremacy in the Persian Gulf.

The occupation of Persia by Russia would be followed by the decline of our trade with the former country, for Russia would take care to strangle any commercial interests that rivalled her own. The trade of Northern India with Central Asia has been killed. An attempt has been made to cripple that between India and Eastern Persia. The crippling of the trade of India would not only be

[1] Captain Mahan in the *National Review* for September, 1902.

disastrous from the commercial point of view, but it would also have a certain effect on our military efficiency, because the Persian trade in Turkoman, Arab, and Persian horses, exported to Quetta, Karachi, and Bombay, though by no means so considerable as it was some years ago, is no negligible quantity.   Our Indian cavalry are not, it is true, now mounted on such horses to a great extent, but if we are to have mounted infantry in India, they will be useful for that purpose.   A considerable number of the best mules of our mountain batteries also comes from Persia.   Amongst other effects an occupation of Persia by Russia might have had, it would certainly have affected the Indian horse trade appreciably.

But we should lose more than the loss of money which the decline in trade implies.   We should lose what is far more valuable—prestige.   The whole Oriental world would have been convinced of our impotence had we yielded to Russia, and the political situation in India, and in Egypt, would have been made considerably more difficult.

There were three ways by which this particular form of Russian expansion could be met : (1) By an inveterate and unyielding hostility to Russian expansion ; (2) by opposition, followed by a graceful climbing down ; (3) by compromise, in which mutual interests were considered.   The second course is one which, however often it has been followed, could never be advised.   The first implies increased naval and military expenditure, a protracted war, and the occupation of further territory by Great Britain. We do not desire to enter on either of these alternatives. It would be better to support Persia as far as possible against Russian aggression ; to meet Russian methods of protection in one part of the country by definitely adopting a similar attitude ourselves in another part ; to meet strategical railway construction by similar counter-construction within our sphere of influence. For example, Russia's advance on the western side might be met by a British railway from Shuster on the Karun to Isfahan. As has already been mentioned, a good road, with iron bridges, has lately been completed between these two points by the private enterprise of British merchants, and a water route up to Shuster has also been established by the same agency. Her advance on the eastern side might be met by the extension of the railway from Quetta to Nushki and Robat. It is possible that eventually these two lines, with rail-heads at Robat and Isfahan, may be linked up by Kerman and Yezd. The railway would probably be a commercial success, and would certainly be invaluable in war, when its position would be protected to a great extent by the Dasht-i-Lut. By this means, too, we should develop that most fertile of provinces, Seistan, make it an open market to British-Indian trade, and establish a potential base there which would lie across Russia's easiest path of advance to the Arabian Sea, should she ever come down with the design of creating a new Port Arthur in those waters. Lord Ronaldshay says that the Ameer of Seistan spoke with assurance of the advantage of a line from Quetta to Robat, which he looked upon as "a certain production of the near future."[1]

We should, in fact, adopt the third course. This has been done, and the Anglo-Russian Convention, which we will proceed to discuss, is the outcome of negotiations with that end in view.

THE ANGLO-RUSSIAN CONVENTION

This Convention, signed at St. Petersburg, August 31, 1907, is one of the most interesting we shall have to deal with. It was described in the spring of 1908 by Lord Curzon, in the House of Lords, as the most important and far-reaching which we have signed for fifty years, while Lord Morley (then Mr. Morley), in the House of Commons, characterized it as one of the most momentous ever signed in connection with the defence of our position in India. However such superlatives may appeal to him, no one can deny its importance as a guarantee for the balance of power and the peace of the world.

Two separate agreements, relating respectively to Persia and Tibet, and a convention concerning Afghanistan, are included in the Convention. Their provisions, which were given to Parliament in October, 1907, briefly put, run as follows: That dealing with Persia begins by declaring that the two Powers, having mutually engaged to respect the integrity and independence of that country, and sincerely desiring the preservation of order, peaceful development, and the establishment of

---

[1] *Sport and Politics under an Eastern Sky.* Blackwood.

equal opportunities for the trade and industry of all nations in it, have agreed on the following terms, which specify only those provinces of Persia in which Russia and England have, for geographical and economical reasons, especial interest for the maintenance of peace and order.   Under it Great Britain, on the one hand, engages neither to seek nor to support on behalf of British subjects, or of the subjects of third Powers, any commercial or political concessions, such as railways, banks, telegraphs, roads or transport, or insurance, north of a line drawn from Kasr-i-Shirin on the Turko-Persian frontier, west of Kermanshah, by way of, and including, Isfahan, Yezd, and Khakhk, to the point where the Persian, Russian, and Afghanistan frontiers meet.   Russia makes a corresponding engagement in identical terms within a zone extending over South-Eastern Persia from the Perso-Afghan frontier, by way of, and including, Gazik, Birjand, and Kerman, to Bandar Abbas on the Persian Gulf.   Great Britain will not oppose the granting of concessions to Russian subjects within the former zone, and Russia will act similarly as regards British subjects within the latter.   Existing concessions within these zones are to be maintained.   The customs and other revenues pledged by Persia as security for loans already made by the Russian and British banks are safeguarded by two further articles.   Friendly exchange of ideas in the event of financial difficulties requiring the establishment of a Russian or British control, respectively, over the resources of those revenues is provided for.

As regards the Convention concerning Afghanistan, by the first article Great Britain declares that she has no intention of changing the political status of that country, and undertakes to exercise her influence in Afghanistan solely in a pacific sense, and not to take, or encourage Afghanistan to take, measures which would threaten Russia. On the basis of the Treaty of Kabul, of March 21, 1905, Great Britain engages also not to annex, or to occupy, any part of Afghanistan, or to interfere in its internal administration, so long as the Ameer fulfils the engagements he contracted towards Great Britain under that Treaty. Russia, on the other hand, formally declares Afghanistan to be outside her sphere of influence, undertakes to conduct all her political relations with Afghanistan through the British Government, and pledges herself not to send any agents into Afghanistan. Specially appointed Russian and Afghanistan authorities on the frontier, or in the frontier provinces, may, however, enter into direct relations for the settlement of local and non-political questions. Other provisions, with regard to commerce, will be found in the full text of the Convention, which is given in Appendix I.

As regards Tibet, the agreement recognizes the suzerainty of China over that country, and closes it against both Russia and Great Britain, politically, commercially, and financially, subject to certain limited rights accruing to Great Britain under the Treaty of Lhassa, of 1904, and the Anglo-Chinese Convention, which confirmed that Treaty in 1906.

That a document so momentous should receive severe criticism is, of course, inevitable. That some of this criticism must be unanswerable is evident,

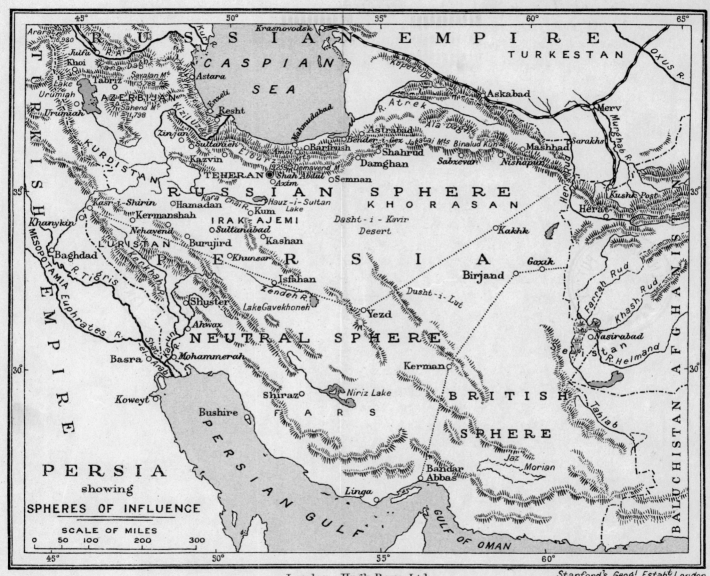

PERSIA
showing
SPHERES OF INFLUENCE

SCALE OF MILES
0   50 100   200   300

London : Hugh Rees, Ltd.

Stanford's Geogl. Estabt, London.

because such a Convention could only have been arrived at by a process of compromise, and compromises demand concessions from both parties. A dispassionate observer of what has been going on for years will arrive at the conclusion that the situation was such that some means of establishing an understanding with regard to it was absolutely necessary, and that the policy of drift, which we had followed in the past with much loyalty to our traditions, could not continue to guide us in the future without serious danger. Had we not drifted in years gone by, and declined to give Persia financial assistance[1]—sought from us and obtained from Russia—we should have been in a better position to make terms. As it was, when the Convention was agreed to, the military preponderance of Russia in the north of Persia was supplemented by the power of the purse which she had gained by our hesitation. The power of the purse, and the power of the sword, potent up to Teheran, were obstacles and realities which we had to face. They were the assets, from the diplomatic point of view, of which Russia was in possession. The time came when we had to seek for advantages to counterbalance them.

But beyond and above the securing of advantages, either commercial or military, it was essential to establish friendly relations between England and Russia in the Middle East. Both great parties of the State have shown themselves sensible of this, and the dispute which has raged

---

[1] In 1898 the British Government refused to guarantee a loan of £2,500,000 to Persia.

round this Convention concerns itself not so much with the necessity for some such agreement as with the terms by which this country purchased it. On the whole it may be said that the admitted dangers of conventions such as we are discussing should not have frightened us from attempting to make this one, and a dispassionate view of the whole situation has revealed greater probabilities of benefit than of disadvantage.   While we have been generous in our confidence, it has yet to be shown that we have not been wise.   In political as well as personal matters confidence is a plant of slow growth.   We can scarcely be surprised, then, if the attempt to make mutual confidence a factor of stability in international affairs should be received with some suspicion.

To the soldier, the strategic concessions which we have obtained in Seistan and Persian Baluchistan will be of main interest.   Geography is intimately connected with these strategic concessions, because the situation of these two countries lies on the exposed flank of our Indian frontier, and an enemy penetrating them would completely turn our line of defence.

Treaties are not usually the product of pure philanthropy.   Self-interest and self-advantage must claim first place—it is even the duty of diplomatists to see that they shall do so.   It is, therefore, not surprising that in our case military considerations connected with the defence of India overshadowed others, and outweighed commercial advantages to ourselves and to Persia which might have accrued from any treaty we might have made.

To secure as sound a strategical position as possible
we had to make concessions, for obviously Russia
was not going to make a treaty to benefit us alone.
The predominance of our interest in Seistan was
essential, and we have secured that predominance.
To gain our point we have had to make concessions as regards commercial advantages in Persia,
we have had to make concessions in connection
with Afghanistan, and, as regards Tibet, we have
put ourselves under a self-denying ordinance on the
same footing as Russia.   But we have gained this
indisputable advantage, that we can prevent the
construction by Russia in time of peace of a railway in Seistan, which would give her an alternate
line of advance on India should she ever undertake
the invasion of that country.   Of course, it is open to
argument whether the value of that strategical and
military advantage has not been overrated.   The
lines of advance on India are discussed later, and
from what has been said it will not be overlooked that
geographical conditions render the line of advance
just indicated scarcely the one most likely to be
selected ; but to have disposed of one line of advance
out of four remains no small diplomatic achievement, and will, in the event of hostilities in the
future, certainly relieve anxiety.

That a friendly agreement should have been
arrived at with Russia is a gain of most vital
importance.   In addition to that, a considerable
military advantage on the frontier of India has
been obtained ; we have placed on record our
settled policy with regard to Afghanistan, and
have at length obtained a solemn pledge from

Russia that Afghanistan lies outside her sphere of influence.

One feature remarkable about this Convention, to which attention has naturally been drawn by its critics, is that in the body of the agreement no reference is made to the Persian Gulf. This exclusion has been justified on the ground that in an agreement with Russia no stipulation could have been extended beyond the Persian shores, that our interests are not limited by those shores, and that in future, should they become more important in other parts of the Gulf, they might have been weakened had we confined ourselves to such definition of them as alone would have been possible in a convention with Russia. A letter from our Foreign Secretary to our Ambassador in St. Petersburg, however, asserts that Great Britain does not in any way relax her previous claims to the supremacy over the waters of the Gulf, and that Russia recognizes our interests there.

CHAPTER X

AFGHANISTAN AND THE NORTH-WEST FRONTIER OF INDIA

AFGHANISTAN lies between parallels 29° and 38° 20′ of north latitude, and 61° and 72° east longitude, extending with Wakhan, a long narrow tongue of land, to 75° east longitude.

Its boundary with Russian Turkistan follows a line running generally westward from the extreme north-east corner of Lake Victoria, thence along the line of that branch of the Oxus which issues from the Lake, and on along the course of the river to Khamiab. From Khamiab the frontier runs south-west to Zulfikar on the Hari-Rud, and thence south to Koh-i-Malik Siah, where the frontiers of Persia, Afghanistan, and Baluchistan meet. Here the boundary turns round and doubles back eastwardly to the Khwaja Amran range. Until 1893 much uncertainty existed as to the eastern and southern boundaries, but in that year a conference between the Ameer Abdur Rahman and Sir Mortimer Durand was held, and a boundary agreed upon, which is now demarcated with the exception of the Khaibar-Asmar section. The Ameer allowed Chitral, Bajaor and Swat to be included within the British sphere of influence, while he retained Asmar, the Kunar Valley above it, as far as Arnawai, and the tract of Birmal west of Waziristan. In the subsequent demarcation Kafiristan was included within the sphere of Afghan control, while on the other hand the Ameer withdrew his pretensions to Waziristan.

Afghanistan measures nearly 600 miles from its eastern to its western frontier, and is about 500 miles in breadth from north to south. Its area is about 250,000 square miles. It impinges on the north with the Central Asian States under the influence of Russia, on the west it marches with Persia, on the south with British Baluchistan, and on the east with the North-West Frontier Province. The mountain tribes scattered along the north-west frontier of India are included within this Province.

After the second Afghan war in the summer of 1880 Kabul and Kandahar were held by British troops. The British Government then offered the Ameership of Kabul to Abdur Rahman, and when he accepted it withdrew the British forces. It was agreed with Abdur Rahman that the British Government was to have control of his relations with foreign States, who, on their part, undertook not to interfere with the internal government of Afghanistan. In the case of unprovoked foreign aggression on Afghanistan dominions, the British Government agreed to aid the Ameer in such manner as it might deem necessary, always provided that he unreservedly followed their advice in regard to his external relations. In 1893 this position was confirmed, and a formal treaty was signed in March, 1905, by which the present Ameer, Habibulla Khan, accepted unreservedly the engagements which his father Abdur Rahman had entered into with the British Government. By the Anglo-Russian Convention of 1907 Great Britain enters into certain engagements with regard to Afghanistan, which are mentioned on p. 259.

Afghan territory is politically divided into the four provinces of Kabul, Turkistan, Herat and Kandahar, Badakshan being now absorbed in Turkistan. Each province is under a Hakim, or Governor (called Naib), under whom justice is dispensed after a feudal fashion.

The population of the country is from four to five millions, the dominant race being Durranis, the most numerous the Ghilzais, of whom there are at least a million. There are also Tajiks, Hazaras, Aimaks and Uzbeks. The Tajiks are scattered all over the country, are undoubtedly the original Persian stock, and prefer agricultural and industrial occupations. The Ghilzais occupy the country south-east of Kabul, and also that between Kabul and Kandahar, while the Durranis inhabit the northern slopes of the Koh-i-Safed and Western Afghanistan. The Hazaras, who are probably of Tartar extraction, occupy the highlands of that name, and are also found with Aimaks in the Paropamisus Mountains. With the exception of this tribe, which consists chiefly of Shiahs, and of another tribe, the inhabitants are Mohammedans of the Sunni sect.

The revenue of the country fluctuates very

considerably, and it is not possible to specify the
present revenue exactly. What is certain is that
the Ameer receives a subsidy from the Indian
Government originally fixed at Rx. 120,000, but
increased in 1893 to Rx. 180,000, a year. Including subsidy, his total revenue has been estimated at
between twelve to thirteen millions of rupees of
British currency, but this estimate is probably
too low.

No trustworthy statistics regarding the strength
of the Afghan army are available. It is supposed to
number between 60,000 and 90,000 men, including
9,000 cavalry, and 360 guns, but it is supplemented
by large local levies of horse and foot. Herat,
Mazar-i-Sharif, Kandahar, Jelalabad, Kabul, Asmar,
and some other places, are garrisoned by regular
troops. Artillery, rifles and ammunition are manu-
factured in an arsenal at Kabul under the super-
intendence of Europeans in the Ameer's service.
In 1902, with the approval of the Indian Government, the Ameer obtained thirty machine-guns and
howitzers from Essen. Large numbers of fire-
arms are smuggled through Persia, and the tribesmen eagerly purchase them, but it is estimated
that the State possesses, in addition, enough breech-
loading rifles to arm 100,000 infantry.

There are two harvests in the year in most parts
of Afghanistan—one, sown at the end of autumn
and reaped in the summer, consisting chiefly of
wheat and barley, with some peas and beans; the
other, sown at the end of spring and reaped in
autumn, consists of rice, millet, arzna, Indian corn,
etc. Fruit and plants used in the manufacture of

drugs are produced in great abundance. Copper is said to exist in considerable quantities in Northern Afghanistan, and lead is found in many parts. The manufacture of silk, felt, felt overcoats, carpets, garments and shawls from camels' and goats' hair, forms the principal industries. The manufacture of sheepskin *postins* is one of the most important.

The trade routes of Afghanistan run as follows —From Persia by Mashad to Herat. From Bokhara by Merv to Herat. From Bokhara by Karchi, Mazar-i-Sharif and Khulm to Kabul. From East Turkistan by Chitral and the Khawak Pass to Jelalabad. From India by the Khaibar and Abkhana roads to Kabul. From India by the Gomal Pass to Ghazni. From Chaman to Kandahar and thence to Kabul or Herat.

The roads are few in number. The Khaibar and Bolan roads are, however, excellent, and fit for wheeled traffic as far as Kabul and Kandahar, respectively. No wheeled traffic is made use of in the country, however, merchandise being carried on pony or camel back.

There are practically no navigable rivers in Afghanistan. Timber is the only article of commerce conveyed by water, and is floated downstream in rafts.

Such are a few brief details as to the country, but it is in connection with the defence of the North-West Frontier of India that Afghanistan has a special interest for British officers, and should become an object of their study. Moreover, it is by the standard which the defence of that frontier demands that the size of our regular army is to be measured, for many responsible statesmen regard it as defining the utmost strain which can be put on our resources. If we are equal to maintaining ourselves in a war for the North-West Frontier of India, we are presumed to be equal to any crisis which at present it is probable that we may have to face.

This most important, therefore, of our frontiers is remarkable because, unlike most frontiers, it has to be considered with reference to three lines of demarcation—that is to say, the line of the administrative frontier of British India, the line drawn by the Durand Agreement with the Ameer Abdur Rahman in 1893, which delimited the eastern and southern frontier of Afghanistan from Wakhan to Persia, and the border of Afghanistan which, as has been pointed out when dealing with frontiers, may be regarded as our advanced strategical frontier. But what we term the North-West Frontier of India, or rather the line of defence along it, as will be seen from the accompanying map, runs as follows :

From the mountainous country south and east of the Shandur range, which includes Hunza, Gilgit, Chitral, Bajaor, Swat, Buner, part of the Kabul River and Khaibar Pass, the Koh-i-Safed, the Kuram River and Pass, the Tochi River with its Pass, through Waziristan, across the Gomal River and Pass, to the country of the Baluch tribes bordered on the east by the Suleiman Mountains and the Bolan Pass. Then the Kirthar range and the hills and valleys of Baluchistan carry it into the Arabian Sea a little west of Karachi.

Examining this line from right to left, we observe that it is furnished with many routes and passes, that of these some are closed in winter, some are otherwise impracticable, and that only a few, which will be considered later on, permit of the passage of great modern armies.

To consider the defence of a frontier, in the first place it is necessary to study the lines by which it may be approached.   An examination of the line just indicated will show us that the avenues by which Russia (who, if not just at present, may some day give us trouble) could advance upon India are four. That is to say, on the extreme north, the approach from the Pamirs through Chitral or Gilgit ; next to it, southwards, the line from Samarkand via Mazar-i-Sharif and Kabul; again progressing southwards, the line from Merv and Khushk via Herat and Kandahar ; and finally, on the extreme south-west, an advance through Southern Baluchistan.   Of these, the first line is not likely to be adopted, although it is said the Russians pay attention to it.   It leads through a country probably too difficult to be selected for such an enterprise.   On the other hand, the line on the extreme south-west, which formerly had to be considered, can now be left out of calculation, because, as has been shown, it has been neutralized by the Anglo-Russian Convention with regard to Persia.

The approaches by which India can be invaded by Russia are, therefore, practically reduced to two —that is to say, the one which may be termed the Kandahar route, and the other which leads through Kabul.   Many high authorities regard the former as the more probable one, and it has undoubted advantages. But it has also disadvantages, which we must consider before coming to a conclusion.

As has been noted briefly when deserts as frontiers were under discussion, this line of advance, supposing the invader to have succeeded in forcing his way past Quetta, would land him in a difficult position from which to undertake the subjugation of India. He would emerge from the inhospitable country on the right bank of the Indus into a region which would be of little strategical value, and which could not be made to contribute towards the accumulation of supplies that invasion by a large army would necessitate. He would have to the south on his right flank Karachi, a port into which we might pour reinforcements from home, or troops drawn from other parts of India. To the east would lie the great Scinde Desert. Having, therefore, forced the door, he would be still far removed from the strategical points on which the equilibrium of Indian resources, political and military, is poised. Therefore, in spite of the fact that railway construction from Khushk via Herat towards Kandahar would be far easier than by the northern line of advance, the disadvantages just mentioned may very probably outweigh other considerations when an invader has to make his choice.

We may now proceed to examine the railway systems which will assist the advance of Russia.

An invasion of India without lines of rail behind it can no longer be regarded as possible. It is true that in former days the great conquerors who descended on her plains succeeded in carrying great armies of men over passes and through regions now regarded as impracticable. If Alexander, advancing with his main body by the Kaoshan Pass and Kabul River, while he pushed his left through the Swat and Buner districts, could provide for his many fighting men, and Timurlane, marching by the Khawak Pass, did not find the task of feeding his horses impossible, why, it may be asked, should we so regard these tasks now? The reply is that the armies of the ancients did not rely on ball ammunition and shells; they had no magazine rifles and no quick-firing guns with that voracious appetite for ammunition which distinguishes our weapons; they carried few or no medical comforts for the men, and the question of feeding was comparatively simple when soldiers' appetites were more easily provided for, or less considered, than in these degenerate days. The question of supply now dominates all operations, and where vast armies are concerned it is a compelling one. Russia will not be able to dispense with a railway, and the war for the Indian frontier will once more illustrate the fact that in a great war it is excellence of transport and communications which, in the long-run, give victory. Now, there are two railway lines which will enormously facilitate the invasion of India from the north—that running in connection with a service of steamers across the Caspian to Krasnovodsk and Mikhailovsk and on via Merv to Khushk; the other, that connected with the great Siberian Railway at Samara, north-west of Orenberg, and running east of the Sea of Aral along the valley of the Syr Daria or Jaxartes to Tashkent and Samar-

kand.   It is extended thence across the Amu Daria
or Oxus at Charjui to Merv, while it is pushed
eastwards to Khojent, Khokand, and Andijan.
Khushk is only some seventy miles north of Herat,
while it was stated by a correspondent of the *Times
of India*, in April, 1905, that a new branch line is
being made from Samarkand due south to Tarmes
on the Oxus, opposite Balkh.[1]   Sir Edward Collen,
however, considers that this line will have to make
a wide sweep from the direct line south in order to
avoid a hilly and difficult country.

Having regard to the lines of advance that seem
most favourable to Russia, we may now consider
the country which will, in all probability, form the
theatre of operations.

There was formerly an idea that the true defence
of India should consist in an occupation of the
line of the Indus and the assumption of a passive
attitude.   The best military authorities have now,
however, abandoned this view, and, in any case, it
is utterly obsolete since we have guaranteed the
integrity of Afghanistan.   It is for Afghanistan
and in Afghanistan that we shall have to fight.
It is the terrain of that country which we should
study.   Considered as a theatre of operations it may
be divided into four great divisions.   The first, a
mass of mountainous country on the east ; the
second, the hilly country and plains of Afghan
Turkistan on the north, which are comparatively
fertile ; the third, the mountainous country enclosed in the triangle Kabul, Kandahar, and

---

[1] Quoted by the *Times* military correspondent on May 15, 1905, in
an article in that paper.

Herat ; and, lastly, the desert country of the Helmand basin, and Baluchistan.[1] What is especially noticeable and interesting to us is the general height of Afghanistan above the plains of India, while the most striking feature in the country is the great dividing line of the Hindu Kush. The country gradually slopes upward from south-west to north-east, and this will be better appreciated by remembering that, while Kabul is some 7,300 feet above the sea-level, Kandahar is only about 3,300 feet, and Herat 2,500 feet, above it. Spurs of the enormous range of the Hindu Kush are to be recognized in the Gul Koh, through Ghazni, in the Hazara highlands, in the Koh-i-Safed on the southern bank of the Hari-Rud, in the Paropamisus, and in the northern Highlands of Afghan-Turkistan. On the extreme east this massive Hindu Kush forms a great barrier to hostile enterprise. The Kilik Pass at 15,600 feet, the Baroghil at 12,400, the Dorah Pass at 14,800, and others of lesser importance, can be crossed by small parties when they are not under deep snow. But the difficulties of these routes are deterrent, and with the measures of protection that have been adopted we may feel fairly well assured that we could block any small column an adventurous invader might push forward, whether towards Gilgit or to Chitral, and so by the Kunar Valley to Jelalabad, or by the route into the Swat Valley. The group of passes we have especially to consider

---

[1] *The Defence of India,* by General Sir Edwin Collen, G.C.I.E. London, printed for His Majesty's Stationery Office by Harrison and Sons, 1906.

are those that lie between the Khawak Pass and Irak Pass in the Koh-i-baba. The Khawak Pass itself can be traversed by caravans at 11,600 feet, and leads from Afghan Turkistan into the Panjshir Valley. The interval between it and the Irak Pass is about 150 miles, and in it the principal passes are the Kaoshan, 14,300 feet, and the Chahardar, 13,900 feet. Kaoshan was the pass used by Alexander the Great, and it also constituted the highway of the successive hosts which have swept down upon Kabul and India. But there are other lesser passes, which have been improved artificially, and the great height of the Kaoshan renders it extremely difficult. The route by the Chahardar Pass was made by the late Ameer Abdur Rahman, and turns south into the Ghorband Valley, but it is almost impassable in winter, even for small parties of men. The route through the Valley of Bamian by the Irak Pass to Kabul is well known, and has been improved of late years. But the hills extend northwards to Mazar-i-Sharif, Tashkurghan, and Kunduz, and the roads leading to the Hindu Kush from these places traverse a wild country of rocks, defiles, and gorges. Some 250 miles lie between Kabul and Mazar-i-Sharif. The former place is divided from Tashkurghan by 276 miles, or 250 miles by the Chahardar Pass. Along the line of hills from Bamian to Herat there is nothing that can be called a road practicable for an army heading southwards from the Oxus.

At the other extremity of our line a more favourable state of things is seen: the country is less barren; the natural obstructions fewer. Herat, if no modern fortress, is now far stronger than it used to be. It could not be taken by a *coup de main*, and with a garrison staunch and well commanded is capable of standing a siege of some months. Until comparatively late years Herat has often been spoken of as the key of India. If never the key, it was certainly the gate, because it is a rich province, in which cereals could be grown to provide for a concentration of troops, and where a good advanced base for the attack of India could be established. It is undoubtedly a strategical point of importance. It is connected by trade routes with the principal towns of all the neighbouring territories: with Kabul through the depression of the Hari-Rud; with Mazar-i-Sharif and Bokhara through Maimana; with Khiva through Merv; with Mashad, Seistan, and Kandahar. It possesses a good climate and lies in a fertile valley. In almost all the older projects for the attack of India, it was assumed that the place of starting of the invader would be Herat. But the commercial valley of Herat is at present by no means what it was, thanks to the progress of railway communications which have been made on the other great commercial highways of Asia. "It is its river, and the irrigation which it brings with it, that now gives it commercial importance, and because of the fertility with which it is endowed."[1] Centuries ago, when the Turk blocked the direct trade route from east to west, commerce flowed by Herat, Tiflis, and the Black Sea; and, again, another route ran southwards to Kandahar and Multan. Herat

[1] *The Indian Borderland*, by Sir T. Holdich.

14—2

was then a centre of the highest commercial importance. The sea route to India has, however, put it in the shade with respect to its commercial position on the one hand, while on the other railways have modified both the strategical situation and its importance as a source of supplies.

Even if Russia were to lay siege to Herat, it will, in the eyes of many, become a question whether or not we should push forward and relieve it. It is an even more difficult problem whether, supposing Russia to have gained possession, we should advance and endeavour to turn her out. Should we, in fact, await the attack of Russia at Kandahar, or go forward with the idea of driving her back from Herat? An important factor in the question formerly was the attitude of the Afghans. At present there ought to be no question as to that, for not only have we a distinct alliance with them guaranteeing the integrity of their country, and our aid in its preservation, but by the recent Anglo-Russian Convention the integrity of Afghanistan is doubly safeguarded. It is, nevertheless, not by any means certain that we should be welcomed as deliverers by proud inhabitants; and, in spite of conventions and treaties, their attitude will have to be reckoned with. The distance from Herat to Kandahar is some 400 miles, and such a length of route would hamper our freedom of movement and weaken our forces by all that a long line of communications implies. To advance against Russia on the other flank would have this disadvantage, that Russia might fall back before us and elude our blow, and that there is no strategical point within reasonable reach of sufficient importance to compel her to fight a decisive battle for its protection.   We might, therefore, by making an advance on the Kabul side, strike a blow in the ear, and be met by Russia's traditional policy of evasion and making space her ally.

Southwards from Herat a route runs by Sabzawar to Farah, then bends by an obtuse angle to Girishk, and through it to Kandahar.   Between Herat and Farah lie open undulating ground and small low hills.   From Farah to Girishk on the Helmand the roadway is fairly level, and for part of the way is flanked by the Zamindawar Hills, which are the stronghold of the Ghazis.   There exists at Girishk a position which is very strong, and an invader would come upon it at the end of a long line of communications, to guard which his fighting force would have to be denuded of many rifles.   It is by this well-known position that Kandahar is covered from the north-west.   Between it and that city there is no obstacle of any importance, but Kandahar itself offers opportunity for defence, and at Quetta, behind it, there lies a position of extraordinary natural strength.   All routes south of Herat lead to Quetta.   Quetta could not be conquered by a force marching by Seistan, or even by a line within easy reach of the coast, were such a line a practicable one.[1]   Quetta and Kandahar on one side, and Kabul on the other, are, indeed, the keys to the front door of India.   If we decided

[1] *The Indian Borderland,* by Sir T. Holdich.

to make the neighbourhood of Kandahar our battle-field, the railway might easily be prolonged from New Chaman to Kandahar, or beyond, and would obviate many difficulties of transport. This question of railway extension is one which will again be reverted to. There can, however, be little doubt that, whatever occurred at Herat, and whether we decided to advance on that city or not, the Indian frontier must be defended by holding Kandahar, and that when once Russia had taken any step that constituted an act of war, we should have to reply by occupying that city and the general line between it and Kabul.

Now let us examine for a moment the geographical features of the country that would constitute our strategical front in the event of hostilities. The tumbled mass of impassable country which is known as the Hazara Highlands is its most remarkable feature, and constitutes an obstacle most inconvenient to the attack. An impracticable rampart in itself, it divides the hostile forces so as to render mutual intercommunication, support, or junction almost impossible. It will force an invading army to operate on widely separated lines, and to incur the risks such a method of operating implies. It supplies, in fact, an excellent illustration of the influence that mountain ranges may have on strategy when they do not constitute a direct obstacle to advance, which has been discussed in a previous chapter. It is true, of course, that the late Ameer made a military road from Kabul to Herat, by Daolat Yar, 500 miles long, but this is only suitable for small bodies, and supplies are difficult to find. Behind this mass of hills, however, there is a good road from Kandahar by Ghazni to Kabul, offering lateral communication to the defence, which was utilized by our generals— Lord Roberts and Sir Donald Stewart—during the last Afghan war. There are, in addition, lines of communication with India which join this road at intermediate points.

All the roads leading from the north to the most flourishing parts of India are dominated by Kabul, Kandahar in its turn commanding all the roads leading to India from the west. It has been recommended by Sir Edwin Collen that large entrenched camps should be erected both at Kandahar and Kabul, and he considered that, assisted by Afghans, we could successfully defend that part of our strategic front, while on the south and west we should take advantage of the position on the flank of the Russian advance, which the occupation of Seistan would offer to us.

The extension of the railway, which at present runs as far as Nushki, to Robat and Seistan should be only a matter of time, and Seistan is of potential value, not only as a strategical point on the flank of a Russian advance, but also as a great granary and depot of supplies. When, however, a strategic front extends over such a distance as 300 miles, it must be furnished with a railway, if all the strategical advantages which it offers are to be reaped. The possession of interior lines, which would be ours in this case, can only be fully turned to account when the throwing of troops into the scale from one side to the other, as the situation may demand, can be rapidly accomplished. Lord Roberts, in *Forty-one Years in India*, has told us how he insisted on the necessity for such communications. At present the railway which would furnish us with swift means of movement does not exist, nor have other railways through the Gomal and Zhob valleys to Quetta, and through the Tochi valley to Ghazni, yet been constructed, though they have been recommended by some authorities for many years. Some years ago a survey of the Gomal and Zhob valleys was made, but so far our efforts have ended with it. If strategy and strategical geography were the only points to be considered, no doubt Kabul would already be connected with India by a railway; we should very probably be in railway communication with Kandahar, and the other necessary strategical railways would have been finished by now. But practical politics have stood in the way of railway building, and for good reasons. The Afghans have strong conservative tendencies and a rooted objection to the construction of railways, and it is most undesirable at present to imperil the good relations which exist between us by bringing forward proposals that might be misinterpreted. There are diplomatic reasons, too, for not taking steps towards pushing railways forward unless it becomes absolutely necessary to do so.

An examination of the possible lines of advance by Russia has shown that no invasion of Afghanistan in force by her is possible without the assistance of railways. It has been publicly stated in the House of Commons by Mr. Balfour, speaking as President of the Committee of Imperial Defence,[1] that in order to reach Kabul, Russia would have to cope with no less than 200 miles of mountain, where rock-cutting and other laborious processes would have to be undertaken.   And she would have to enter on this task in the face of a determined resistance by the people of Afghanistan, who, as has been shown, detest railway-making and railway labourers, and have hitherto been able to preserve the maintenance of their prejudices.

The establishment of Afghanistan as a buffer-State, and a buffer-State, too, most difficult to traverse, gives us considerable security, even if its strategical preparation have not all the perfection we may desire.   That inhospitable region has been well described as a country in which a large army would starve, while a small one would be annihilated.   Nor can such a description be regarded as an exaggeration when it is remembered that Lord Roberts officially informed our Defence Committee that he had the utmost difficulty in feeding 12,000 British troops for the eight or nine months during which he was in occupation of Kabul.

Difficulties similar, if not quite so great, would be encountered by an invader who approached India by the route from Herat to Kandahar, and therefore it is a certainty that India cannot be rushed. The safety of India depends, in fact, to a very large extent, on geographical conditions.   Questions must be solved connected not only with difficulties of route, with obstacles and with lines of communication, but with the resources of the regions that form

[1] Speech in the House of Commons, May 11, 1905.

the anticipated theatre of war, before an advance
can be launched. The quartermaster-general of an
army must satisfy himself as to problems connected
with water-supply, and means of transport, and as
to many other details before invasion is undertaken.

Owing to these geographical difficulties, we must
have ample warning of any effective advance by
Russia. An advance to be effective means an
advance accompanied by a railway, and therefore
it was proposed by Mr. Balfour, in the speech on
the occasion already referred to, that as transport
is the great difficulty of an invading army, we should
not allow anything to be done which would facilitate transport.   In his opinion, it should be considered an act of direct aggression upon India if
any attempt should be made to build a line in connection with Russia's strategic railways within the
territory of Afghanistan. On such an act of aggression taking place, we should, as has been indicated,
probably be compelled to occupy the strategical
front Kabul–Kandahar, the frontier of India would
have to be reconsidered, and so would the strength
of the garrison by which we hold our great possession.   Some authorities, indeed, have considered
that the dividing-line between India and Turkistan
lies along the Hindu Kush and the Hazara Highlands, and would not regard it as unsatisfactory if
Southern Afghanistan marched with Russian territory along that line.   Such a frontier would, however, mean a large addition to the garrison of India,
a greatly enhanced expense, and a drain on our
Indian treasury to be regarded with dismay.

The real danger which formerly existed was

that Russia might gradually absorb the whole of Afghanistan, as she had absorbed the Khanates and the North of Persia. Building railways and making communications good behind her on one pretext or another, she might bring stores from her European bases, cause towns to spring up, create markets, and eventually produce supplies. In other words, she might act as she is doing in Siberia, and by colonizing prepare a starting-point from which the stride to India would be immensely shortened. Thanks to the Anglo-Russian Convention, thanks to the firm language used by Mr. Balfour, it will be rash folly if this insidious advance is ever allowed to take place. Those 200 miles of difficult country on the northern route, those 400 miles of sandy desert on the southern, cannot be neutralized by a railway or traversed by marching in anything but a considerable time. No sudden inroad can now rush India, and railway construction will govern the issue of a war for its possession. In other words, preparation of the theatre of operations, which falls within the province of peace strategy, will go far to determine the result of a war on the Indian frontier just as has been the case when frontiers nearer home were concerned.

CHAPTER XI

ABYSSINIA

LITTLE more than a hundred years ago our fore-fathers read *Rasselas*, and associated it with an almost legendary country, yet forty years ago we conducted a highly successful war ourselves in that country, and twelve years ago, for the first time in history, a European army of 20,000 men was there destroyed. Though to-day it is in closest touch with us through Egypt and the Soudan, mystery invests its strange inhabitants, who, of Semitic origin, have a dark skin, are guided by feudal institutions not dissimilar to those that once obtained in England, were Christians when we were pagans, and are still a coming race though powerful thousands of years ago. And yet the mountains of Abyssinia were always within sight of our ships plying with the East.

To-day, however, our interest in Abyssinia, its people, and its politics is by no means sentimental, but most material and pressing. Between the Egyptian Soudan and Somaliland, confronting Aden, coveted by other nations, watched and nursed by diplomatists, with a population divided by tribal allegiance, and temporarily held together

by the personality of an old man, the situation is
one big with future developments for ourselves, our
allies and friends in France and Italy.

Abyssinia, geographically considered, is a vast
citadel frowning down upon the plains of East

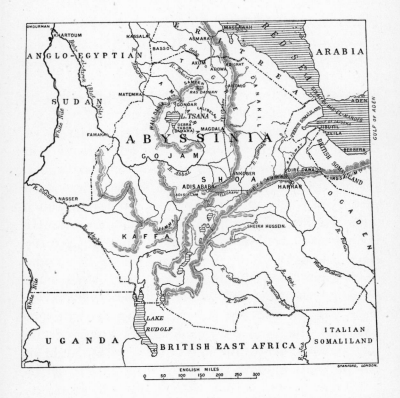

Africa—a great oval mass of mountains forming
a huge rampart, which, crowned with volcanic
peaks, towers 3,000 feet above the shores of the
Red Sea, the plains of Galla, the Egyptian Soudan,
and the deserts that divide Berber and Souakim.

The mountains are steeply scarped on the east,

sloping more gently in broad terraces towards the plains of Nubia, and the valley of the Blue Nile.

Abyssinia is divided into five provinces. Of these, Tigré lies to the north, Amhara forms the centre, while Gojam lies on the south-west, and Shoa on the south, east of Amhara. But there are outlying territories and dependencies, of ill-defined boundaries, as far as Kaffa in the south, and Harrar in the south-east, with considerable portions of the Galla and Somali lands. The whole area is about 200,000 square miles, with a population estimated at from 9,000,000 to 11,000,000.[1]

The most clearly-defined mountain chain is that along the eastern border forming the eastern scarp of the plateau already mentioned, reaching a mean elevation of 7,000 to 8,000 feet. Greater elevations are, however, to be found in the interior, where, in Samien, Ras Dashan reaches 15,158 feet; and in Gojam, where there are mountains only 1,000 feet less in height.

In the north of the country the Atbara rises amid the northern slopes of the mountains round Lake Tsana, and flows to the north till it joins the Nile. From 25 to 40 feet deep in the rains, in the dry season it dwindles to quite an insignificant stream. The Bahr-el-Azrek, better known as the Blue Nile, flows through Lake Tsana, then sweeps round the mountainous province of Gojam in a huge curve, and gathers volume till it mingles with the White Nile at Khartoum, 846 miles away. This is the river that brings to Egypt the fertilizing matter termed " Nile slime," which, deposited in

[1] *Statesman's Year-Book*, 1908.

the valley of the greater river, gives richness to the soil and justifies the phrase " Egypt is the Nile." Any diversion of such a wealth-bearing stream would be fatal to the prosperity of Egypt and the Soudan, and our interest in Abyssinia and its affairs are therefore largely connected with it. The Sobat is hardly to be classed as an Abyssinian river, though its sources lie in the confines of that country, from which it flows in a north-westerly direction till it meets the White Nile as a redoubtable river, 1,000 yards across, and 26 feet deep. Of far less importance than the above are the Omo, which rises in the Jimma Mountains and flows into Lake Rudolf; and the Hawash which, rising in the south-east of Shoa, makes a wide curve the reverse of that described by the White Nile, flows eastwards in considerable volume, yet never reaches the sea, but is lost in the sandy wastes which border the Bay of Tajurra. None of the rivers of Abyssinia are navigable within that country.

In the lower levels of the plateau of Amhara is situated Lake Tsana, a large lake, forty-five miles by twenty-five, and in some places 45 fathoms deep.

The capital of Abyssinia is Adis Abbaba, in Shoa, which has a population of some 10,000. The most important of the other towns are Samara, Adowa (capital of Tigré), Gondar (capital of Amhara), Basso, Axum (the ancient capital of Ethiopia), Ankober (former capital of Shoa), Antalo (former capital of Tigré), and Harrar, which has a population of 40,000, and is some 6,000 feet above the sea.

The most important strategical points are Adowa and Adigrat, in the north ; Ankober and Harrar, in the east; Adis Abbaba, in the south; Nasser, Famaka, Metemma, and Kassala, in the west; and Gondar, Debra-Tabor, and Lalibela, in the interior. All these places control the different approaches to the capital and chief provincial centres, and form depots of supplies at the junctions of the various caravan routes. None are fortified.

There are no roads in Abyssinia; only the tracks followed by caravans and mountain paths. There is, in consequence, no wheeled means of transport. Neither is there any water communication, the rivers being rapid and shallow in summer, and in the winter torrents unsuitable for navigation. They are only bridged in a few places; but, on the other hand, are fordable except during the rainy season.

A railway, of metre gauge, has been built under French auspices from the port of Jibutil to Diré Dawa (about twenty-five miles from Harrar), a distance of 193 miles, and was opened to traffic in 1902. It was originally proposed to build a line of far greater strategical importance, which should connect the Red Sea with the Nile near Fashoda via Diré Dawa and Adis Abbaba. Owing to the elevation of Harrar (6,000 feet), considerable difficulty will be experienced in taking the line to that town, and financial obstacles have stood in the way of the construction of the central and western sections of the railway. It has diverted to Jibutil the Abyssinian trade which used largely to pass to the port of Zeila in British Somaliland, but the camel-drivers of Zeila continue to compete. There are telegraph lines connecting Adis Abbaba with Harrar, with Jibutil, and with Massowah in Eritrea.   Railhead is also connected with Jibutil by telegraph. The telephone system is being extended on the southern frontier.

Its lofty position has given Abyssinia a special climate of its own, or, rather, a variety of climates. Its latitude would class it amongst the hottest regions of the globe, and, in fact, the lower country and deep valleys are very hot and unhealthy.   But the higher plateaus are well watered, and have a genial climate, while, as the mountains are climbed, cold of almost all gradations can be met with. The year may be divided into two seasons—a dry winter and a rainy summer ; but the wet season varies very considerably with the altitude. On the lower zones of the plateau it is most prolonged, while, higher, rain begins to fall earlier, and the rainfall is very heavy—from 30 to 40 inches.[1]

In the hotter regions sugar-cane, cotton, coffee, and bananas flourish ; in the middle zone the vine, maize, wheat, barley, oranges, tobacco, and potatoes are cultivated ; and above 9,000 feet excellent pastures, with some cultivation, are to be found. With regard to local supplies, the country is fairly well provided, and along the main routes cattle and sheep can be purchased in large quantities. In time of war they would probably be driven into the mountains. The corn supply is not plentiful. Wheat and barley can only be bought in the richer valleys in small quantities, as the natives have only enough for themselves. There is very little coal, but plenty of wood, which is used all over the

---

[1] Dr. Martin considers this estimate a low one, and places the rainfall in the highlands at nearer 100 than 40 inches.

country. Cattle, mules, donkeys, camels, goats, and sheep form a large proportion of the wealth of the country. The horses do not reach more than 15 hands, but, though small, are hardy, and are adapted for mounted infantry. The oxen are very powerful, and are kept hard at work, bulls and cows not being put in draught at all. There are several varieties of sheep, but these are usually small, and weigh only from 20 to 30 pounds. Goats are found everywhere throughout the country. Mules, up to 13 hands, are bred everywhere, and used as pack animals. Donkeys are very small, but would make good pack animals, as they carry 200 pounds,[1] including saddle. Camels, chiefly from Somaliland, are strong, healthy, and cheap, carrying loads of 300 pounds.

Until two years ago speculation was rife as to what would happen to this interesting country when Menelek, the present ruler, dies. Whether the French, in alliance with the Russians, would support a candidate of their own for the throne ; whether these countries would work in opposition to us ; and what part Italy would take, were points keenly debated. That there may be rival claimants, uncertainty, and disturbances in the country when the heritage of Menelek has to be apportioned is very possible, but the Powers principally concerned have recently come to an understanding which should obviate the risks of quarrel between them.

Under an agreement, signed December 13, 1906, on behalf of Great Britain, France, and Italy, these

[1] Dr. Martin does not consider that they would carry more than half this load.

three Powers undertake to respect and endeavour to preserve the integrity of Abyssinia ; to act so that industrial concessions made to the one may not injuriously affect the others ; to abstain from intervention in the internal affairs of the country ; and to concert together for the safeguarding of their respective interests in territories bordering on Abyssinia. They further make agreements, as regards railway construction in Abyssinia, for equal treatment in trade and transit. The importation of arms and ammunition is regulated by another agreement of the same date. Thus the chances of war which brooded for some years over the country have been to a great extent dispersed.

The regular army of Abyssinia consists of contingents from the various provinces, and numbers some 150,000 men, which are supplemented by irregulars and by a territorial army. Every man in the regular army is mounted, in theory, if not in practice ; many are armed with Gras and magazine rifles captured from the Italians. Seven batteries of artillery and mitrailleuses, captured at Adowa, are at present in Adis Abbaba.

It was formerly thought probable that when Menelek dies France, Italy, and ourselves would each try to push a candidate. Ras Makonen, who, it was hoped, would be ours, was not so closely connected with the French as Menelek, while he understood and liked us and the Italians.[1] But now Ras Makonen is dead ; Italy, England, and France, who was formerly the danger, will probably agree. France is said to have sent sufficient arms

[1] See Wylde, *Modern Abyssinia*, p. 431.

and ammunition into the country to last for many years, and had not the agreement just referred to been arrived at, she might have brought forward her own candidate, unfriendly to other nations, and thus have caused both Italy and ourselves enormous expense in keeping frontier garrisons for the protection of our spheres of influence both east and west of the country. An unfriendly Abyssinia would also have been a standing menace to a Cape to Cairo railway. Such a danger has, however, been averted, although the interests of France in the country remain considerable. They possess the telephones, telegraphs, postal arrangements (such as they are), and the only railway. The silver coinage is made in France, and the majority of King Menelek's produce is handed over to French subjects to dispose of. There is, however, special promise of a peaceful arrangement in the fact that for the first time in Abyssinian history the reigning Sovereign has nominated his successor. Menelek has named his grandson Tyasus,[1] the son of Ras Michail, who married Menelek's daughter, as heir to the throne, and the preservation of the *status quo* in Abyssinia, if not assured, is at least in sight.

[1] He, with his father, is being sent to visit the principal Courts of Europe.

CHAPTER XII

MANCHURIA

In the preceding chapters many illustrations have been drawn from military history to show the influence of the various branches of geography on both strategy and tactics. These might have been extended to a very great extent, and the part played by geographical factors in determining success or failure in many battles, campaigns, or wars might have been analyzed almost *ad infinitum*. Thus, the conception of the plan of campaign and the progress of operations throughout the long strain of the Peninsular War, or the glorious brevity of the campaign of Waterloo, might have been scrutinized. The triumphs of Napoleon and of Moltke, might all have been dissected, and lessons extracted from every one of them.

An enormous field in the last century alone would, however, have still remained unexplored, and the influences of geography, as has been indicated, cover, not one century, but the history of all wars of which authentic records survive.

Moreover, it is the last great war that has always the strongest attraction for us. Many, perhaps only half of us, believe in the annals that are not attested by living men. Up to our great struggle in South Africa, everything previous to 1870 was ancient history to a large proportion of soldiers. Our experiences in South Africa opened men's eyes. The great principles were vindicated once more. Histories were read during it and after it more than ever. Then the greatest war, as regards magnitude of numbers engaged and precision of weapons employed, which has yet been fought was waged by a nation which had deliberately prepared itself for the struggle by devoted study and attention to professional principles, and science was triumphant. It seems, therefore, not inappropriate to try and gather some lessons from the battlefields of Manchuria, and to note how geographical conditions of all kinds may be shown to have been connected with the origin of the war. A brief sketch, therefore, of the causes that shaped the coming of the strife and influenced its progress will now be given.[1]

In truth, the progress of Russia in Manchuria was influenced, if indeed it might not be said to have been actually created, by geographical influences. Russia for some centuries has been seeking for an ice-free port with an outlet to the ocean. She has probed her way in various directions, but her activities, until the last few years, have been chiefly directed towards the Mediterranean. Time after time, however, her advances towards her traditional goal have been checkmated by the armies or diplomacy of her European neighbours, and she has had to turn her footsteps back.

[1] The writer takes the opportunity of acknowledging the assistance he has received from the history of the struggle compiled by the General Staff at the War Office.

Foiled in the attempt to gain a sea frontier free from ice in Europe, the idea of spreading her Asiatic acquisitions to the shores of the Pacific fired her imagination. Forty-eight years ago, when China had fallen before the allied forces of Great Britain and France, an opportunity presented itself to her. Russia at once turned the weakness of China to account in squeezing from her a treaty by which the eastern coast of Manchuria, from the Amur down to the Korean frontier, became the territory of the Czar. At length Russia seemed to have realized her long-cherished ambition, and to have gained access to an open, even if remote, seaboard.

But clever as this effort of Russian diplomacy was, and vast as were the regions which were thus added to the dominions of her ruler, her dreams were, after all, not completely substantiated. Although the coast-line of the new possessions was washed for many miles by the Sea of Japan, no ice-free port existed on it, and Vladivostok, where the naval headquarters were established, is closed by Nature for three months of the year, although, with much labour and ingenuity, ice-breakers are utilized to keep a passage open, narrow, no doubt, but sufficient for the conveyance of ships of war. Not only that, but other geographical disadvantages attached to the new Russian port. Near to the Pacific, as it was, yet it was not actually on that ocean, and admission to the open sea could only be obtained through the goodwill of Japan. The islanders menaced the two principal avenues which led to complete freedom, just as Turkey and the

Dardanelles blocked her nearer home. On the north-east, between Yeso and the main island of Hondo, the exit is narrowed down to the Tsugaru Channel, while on the south navigation is confined to the narrow straits that divide the southern shore of Korea from the Japanese island of Kiushu. Obviously the Japanese control the northern route, while the southern straits, although 120 miles wide, are broken up by the islands of Tsushima and Ikishima, which constitute serious obstacles to a free passage.

The summit, as often happens, had, after all, not yet been reached. The step forward had merely shown the necessity of yet another stride, and when the diplomatic trophies of 1860 were carried home and examined in cold blood, Russia found herself but little better off than she had been before. To gain freedom of navigation to Vladivostok, Russia discovered that she must establish herself in Southern Korea. To do this she might have made an advance on land, but the step could more easily be accomplished by other means. Several good harbours would be obtained were the island of Tsushima seized in the name of the Czar, and this step was actually taken in 1861. A protest from a British Minister, and the appearance of a British squadron, made Russia again draw in her hand. Her designs, however, were by no means finally abandoned.

In 1885 events on which it is unnecessary to dilate made a port in Eastern waters free from ice throughout the year more necessary than ever to the Czar. Diplomatic efforts were made to secure the lease of Port Lazarev in North-Eastern Korea. Russia declared that she would never occupy Korean territory under any circumstances.

Meanwhile, the insidious approach of Russia had not been without its effect upon Japan. A difference had arisen regarding the ownership of the island of Saghalien, and in 1875 the latter power had been forced to give up the southern half of that island in exchange for the Kurile group of islands, which were in fact already her own.

When the danger that Russia might occupy Korea became imminent, Japan had to choose between two alternatives, neither of which were free from difficulty. Either she must forestall Russia in Korea or she must take steps to free that kingdom from the suzerainty of China, and render it independent. When an attempt was made to assassinate the Korean King and Queen, the unexpected incident gave Japan an opportunity for making a first effort towards recognizing the independence of Korea; but China took measures to regain her former influence, and in 1882 sent troops for the protection of the royal family, thus once more asserting her ascendancy at Seoul. In a few months, however, disturbances in the capital occurred, the Japanese Legation was burnt, and the Tokio Government despatched a force to Seoul, and demanded reparation. The disturbances led to further complications, and war between China and Japan seemed imminent. In 1885, however, the Convention of Tientsin was signed, and by its provisions both countries agreed to withdraw their troops from Korea, and agreed that if either Power should in future find it necessary to intervene in that State with armed force, the other should receive due notice, and have the right to send an equal number of troops.

Such agreements not infrequently stave off rather than avert war, and the one under notice was no exception to the rule.   In 1894 a rebellion broke out against the Government of Korea; China came to the assistance of the King, while Japan, in turn, occupied Fusan and Chemulpo. The rebellion was subdued, only to give opportunity for a quarrel between the protectors of the country, and hostilities soon began between them.   China was defeated on April 10.   The treaty of peace, signed at Shimonoseki, recognized the full and complete independence of Korea, ceded Formosa, the Pescadores, and the Liao-tung Peninsula to Japan, and arranged for a war indemnity of more than £25,000,000 to be paid to her.

By this treaty Russia's hopes of securing an ice-free port on the Pacific were shattered, while the power of Japan was materially advanced. Diplomacy was again resorted to.   Russia, France, and Germany presented a note to Japan on April 20, 1895, before the treaty of peace had been ratified, and suggested to her that she should forgo her claim to territory on the mainland, because a lasting peace in the Far East would otherwise be endangered. Japan, faced by such a combination, could not do otherwise than accept the suggestion, and agreed to forgo her claim to the Liao-tung Peninsula, receiving from China nearly £5,000,000 as a set-off.

The unrest in the Far East was therefore due primarily to the geographical conditions of Russia, and incidents connected with geography caused the next movement in the protracted contest. In 1897 Germany secured a footing in Kiao-chao Bay, which, by an ingenious euphemism, was described as a "leasehold." With Kiao-chao in German hands, with Wei-hai-wei held by the Japanese until China had fulfilled her treaty obligations, and with the prospect that Ta-lien-wan, through British representation, might become a treaty port, Russia determined to settle the question of an ice-free port for good.

On March 27, 1898, a convention was concluded with China by which Port Arthur, Ta-lien-wan, and the adjacent waters were leased to Russia for twenty-five years, at the end of which an extension might, by mutual agreement, be arranged. A neutral zone was also created, and Russia was given power to erect forts and other defences. Port Arthur and Ta-lien-wan were occupied on March 28, 1898.

The policy of lease-making was further continued by Great Britain acquiring a ninety-nine years' lease of certain territory on the mainland opposite Hong Kong, while Wei-hai-wei was also to be held by her as long as Port Arthur remained in Russian hands. Early in 1898, too, France had secured a lease of Kuang-chou-wan.

The remaining stages of the road to the great Russo-Japanese War are connected with diplomacy, although they still have a geographical basis. To narrate them in detail would be to trespass on the domain of military history. It may be stated briefly, however, that the Boxer Rising in 1899, and its consequences, caused the Russians to cross the Amur in August and enter Manchuria from different points. By October the whole of that country was practically in Russian hands.

Meanwhile, the Powers had come to terms with China, and had agreed to withdraw their troops from Pekin on September 17, 1901, leaving behind, however, Legation Guards of a total strength of 2,000 men. During 1902 the numbers fell to the limit that had been arranged.

On January 30, 1902, was signed the Anglo-Japanese Agreement,[1] by which the independence and territorial integrity of the Empires of China and Korea, and equal opportunities in those countries for the commerce and industry of all nations, were to be maintained. By it each Power contracted, in the event of either of them becoming involved in war with a third Power in defence of its interests in the extreme East, to maintain strict neutrality and use its efforts to prevent other Powers from joining in hostilities against its ally.

On March 16, 1902, a Franco-Russian declaration expressed the satisfaction of these two Powers in the Anglo-Japanese Agreement, affirmed the fundamental principles of that agreement as the basis of their own policy, but reserved all right as to the means to be adopted in the case of aggressive action on the part of a third Power or of the recurrence of disturbances in China.

On April 8 a treaty between China and Russia

[1] For the terms of this agreement see Appendix II.

was signed, by which Russia consented to withdraw completely from Manchuria. The evacuation
was to be gradual, and to be completed in three
successive periods of six months, or eighteen
months in all from the date of the signature of
the agreement, and during each period a stipulated
section of territory was to be handed back to
China. Russia, at the same time, took occasion
to declare her adhesion to the principles of the
integrity and independence of China.

The scheme of evacuation was not, however,
carried out, and fresh demands for concessions
regarding Manchuria were made on China. It is
unnecessary, in a work of this kind, to follow the
tortuous and slow course of the diplomacy which
succeeded. Protests from the representatives of
Great Britain and the United States and Japan
were lodged against these new demands of Russia.
A strong anti-Japanese party meanwhile grew up
in Korea, unrest was created, and on October 8,
1895, the Queen was assassinated. About nine
months later the King took refuge in the Russian
Legation. Russia and Japan again arranged to
co-operate in preserving order in the country.

In April, 1898, the Russian and Japanese
Governments again definitely recognized the independence of Korea in a further agreement, by
which they pledged themselves mutually to abstain
from direct interference in that country.

Matters, however, did not progress smoothly,
and aggressive Russian actions affected not only
Manchuria, but Northern Korea too. Finally, on
July 28, 1903, the Japanese Minister at St. Peters-

burg was directed to assert the commercial and industrial interests of Japan in Korea, and point out that if Manchuria were absorbed by Russia the integrity of Korea would be menaced. A draft treaty was next drawn up, by which the independence and integrity of the Chinese and Korean Empires were once more secured. Japan's interests were to be recognized as preponderant in Korea, while Russia's special interest in railway construction in Manchuria, and her action for the protection of her various interests in that country, were acknowledged. Other clauses dealt with comparatively minor conditions.

A draft of this treaty was presented at St. Petersburg on August 12, 1903. Counter proposals were issued to Japan two months later, and negotiations, extending from the beginning of October, 1903, till the middle of January, 1904, followed. Finally, on January 13, 1904, Japan stated that she would accept the Russian proposal that Manchuria should be regarded as outside the sphere of Japan's influence, on condition that Russia made a similar engagement as regards Korea. No reply was received, and on February 6 the Japanese Minister at St. Petersburg announced that he had been directed to break off diplomatic relations with Russia and withdraw from the capital.

It will be seen from the preceding narrative that the great Russo-Japanese struggle had its origin in, and was directly brought about by questions connected with geography, and that the ultimate rupture was due to Russia's unwillingness to abandon her claims to a vast tract of country, which she wished to acquire in order to redress the disadvantages under which she was placed by Nature in regard to an ice-free port.

Geography, thus far, had probably affected the high political and diplomatic contest alone. As will be shown, however, considerations connected with physical geography influenced the strategy of the whole campaign. But since in the term geography are included matters far beyond the realm of physical geography alone, it is necessary to touch on another feature of geography, which is a matter of the very first importance in any study of the great war which ensued. When Russia found herself actually at war with Japan, she had practically pitted her rail-power against the sea-power of her enemy. Not that she had taken such a course deliberately, or realized, perhaps, at first the necessary consequences of her action ; she probably imagined that her sea-power was stronger than that of Japan, and that the task before her would, therefore, be immensely easier than it proved to be, since the large forces she already possessed in Manchuria and in Western Siberia behind would be more than a match for any forces the Japanese could bring against her when they were not assured of freedom of transit across the sea. As, however, events turned out, it was railway transport that was ultimately pitted against sea and rail transport, and it is necessary, therefore, for us, in the first place, to examine what the railway resources and communications of Russia from her home centres to the Far East really were.

To feed her army in the coming conflict, and

keep it supplied with all the essentials which modern war demands, Russia was obliged to rely on the Trans-Siberian Railway as far as Harbin and the extension southward to Port Arthur, which her occupation of Manchuria had called into existence. The total length of this line from Moscow to Port Arthur is about 5,500 miles. Not only that, but there was a serious gap at Lake Baikal, where a deviation round the southern shores of the lake did not exist at the beginning of the war, although some months afterwards it was completed. This line of railway was a single one, and it was not regarded in this country before the outbreak of war as by any means an efficient line, even in the class to which it belonged. It had ostensibly been built for commercial as well as strategical reasons. There is no doubt that it was strategical interests that pushed it forward, and it is interesting to note that these strategical interests were satisfied, owing to the astonishing energy and skill of Count Khilkoff, who managed the railway system throughout the war.

The details of the construction of this great line of rail need not be examined here. On the whole it did not constitute a very difficult undertaking, because beyond the Urals the rails were laid in straight lines over limitless plains, and between the Ob and the Yenisei there were only gentle undulations to be overcome. After crossing the Yenisei, a series of hills, never exceeding 2,000 feet in height, are traversed at right angles. In the whole distance from Cheiliabinsk to Irkutsk no tunnel occurs, no steeper gradient than $17\frac{1}{2}$ in

1,000, no curves sharper than 2 in 70 yards are met. Beyond Irkutsk, however, there was difficult work to be done, and, moreover, the deviation round the southern edge of Lake Baikal and the country eastward of it offered serious difficulties. Against this vast work of engineering on which Russian success must depend was opposed the best road in the world, Nature's own highway, the sea. But the right to use this road must be won by force of arms, and the seas that formed a considerable portion of the theatre of war must therefore now be described.

The most important are the Sea of Japan and the Yellow Sea, linked together by the Straits of Korea, and lying east and west of that country. The Pacific can be reached by several avenues from the Sea of Japan. The two most important of these, as has been already mentioned, were practically under Japanese control. But there is a third way, free from ice throughout the year, leading from the ocean through the Straits of Perouse, between the islands of Saghalien and Hokkaido (Yeso).

Between the western coast-line of Korea and the Shantung Province of the Chinese Empire lies the Yellow Sea, at the north-west extremity of which are the Gulfs of Pei-chi-li and Liao-tung. To reach these portions of the sea, the Straits of Pei-chi-li, some sixty miles in width from the Liao-tung Peninsula to a protuberance of the Shan-tung Province, must be traversed. On the northern coast of the Gulf of Liao-tung, and on the left bank of the Liao Ho, about thirteen miles

16

from its mouth, the port of Newchwang, closed for some months of the year by ice, is situated.

Turning once more to the land we find Korea, a purely agricultural and mountainous country, 150 miles in breadth and 400 to 600 miles in length, with an area about equal to that of England and Scotland, stretching out from Manchuria towards the south-western corner of Japan. It possesses excellent ports on the southern and western coasts, and on the east the harbour of Gensan. On the Korean Straits is Masampo, a good port, and forty miles east of it is Fusan, the terminus of the railway to Seoul.

Not far from its south-western extremity lies Mokpo, and further north are the harbours of Chemulpo and Chinampo. The former, on the estuary of the Salie River, is linked to Seoul by a single line of railway twenty-six miles long, and is free from ice except in the winter months. North of Chemulpo is Chinampo, on the right bank of the Tatong River, twenty miles from the sea, and closed for at least two months annually by ice. Forty miles up the river lies Pingyang, a town of 35,000 inhabitants.

Geographically, Japan possessed an immense advantage in that, if she could command the sea, the whole seaboard of the theatre of war lay open to her attack. Her own coast-line, too, possessed many fine harbours, linked with the interior by rail, offering facilities for embarking troops, while the Inland Sea supplies a line of communication sufficiently safe as far as the western extremity of the main island. The 120 miles where the Straits of Korea separate

her from Masampo were more dangerous; but, on
the other hand, Vladivostok and Port Arthur were
rather more than 500 miles distant from the same
point.

Without pausing to discuss the question as to
how these geographical conditions and disadvantages were respectively turned to account, we
may note that at the outset of the war another
geographical question materially affected the first
movements of Japan. Political and strategical considerations made it necessary for her to occupy Seoul
at once and forestall the Russians, to whose interests
it would also be to occupy the Korean capital. If
the Russians could be forestalled in Korea, they
would find it difficult, if not impossible, to secure
a port in the south of that country which would
serve as a base of operations against Japan. On
the other hand, could the Japanese occupy the
country, the harbours on its western coast would be
available as bases for their fleet. The rapid occupation of Korea also offered a further great advantage
to Japan, for she might find it possible to seize the
northern ports quickly, and, by disembarking troops
there, save the long and toilsome march to the Manchurian frontier, which the distance (some 400 miles)
from Fusan on the Korean Straits to the Ya-lu,
would necessitate.

While touching on these geographical features, it
is out of place here to tell the story of the operations which have made them famous, and we will
pass on to examine the geography of the theatre
of operations on shore, and see how far it modified
the strategy and tactics of the combatants.

Roads hardly exist to the interior of Korea, but there are unmetalled tracks, steep and stony, which will permit cavalry, infantry, and mountain artillery to move freely in dry weather, but only with extreme difficulty in wet.

To the north-east of Korea the Russian Maritime Province known as Primorsk is situated, while across the Ya-lu and Tumen Rivers, flowing in opposite directions and forming the frontier, lies Manchuria. The latter forms the north-east corner of the Chinese Empire. It is divided into three provinces, and contains some 366,000 square miles. Operations were confined, however, to Feng-tien and Kirin, which cover only 161,000 square miles, an area slightly greater than that of the Transvaal and Orange River Colony combined.

Mountains and plains, the nature of the soil and its products, river-lines and the frontier of the neighbouring State, all had an important bearing on the operations of the war we are discussing, as will be seen from the following account of the theatre in which they were conducted. The main region, a vast mass of mountains between the Ya-lu and Liao Rivers, stretches from the Liao-tung Peninsula away to the north-east into the Maritime Province, called Primorsk. Several roads lead across it. Operations in this elevated region are as difficult as they usually are in such a country, and are largely confined to roads or tracks. There are, however, of the former, only a few, and of the latter not many more. There is, however, a road from Korea to the Chinese capital by way of Liao-yang, termed the Imperial Peking Highway. It crosses the mountainous region we are discussing by the Motien Ling Pass, at an altitude of 4,000 feet. Farther to the south-west, where the range is lower, there are several other roads, and still farther away, in the same direction, roads across the Peninsula become numerous. The hills are for the most part wooded, more especially so in the higher regions, and the so-called roads across the main ridge are merely cart-tracks, steep and narrow, making the passage of large bodies of troops and transports a slow and arduous undertaking.

To the west of the mass of mountains which we have just described lies a broad plain, being, in fact, the valley of the Liao Ho, and on this alluvial deposit large quantities of millet and beans are grown. Beyond the plain on the western bank of the Liao River the frontier of the neutral province of Mongolia is reached. The theatre of operations, therefore, lay between the boundary of a neutral State and a mountainous region in which mobility was much curtailed. In the valley conditions more favourable to movement existed, but the immense crops of millet, which is planted in drills 2 feet apart, and grows to as much as 12 to 15 feet in height, obscure the view, obstruct evolutions, and act as a screen to the movement of troops. Further, by breaking off the stalks some 3 feet from the ground an obstacle rendering the ground wellnigh impassable for troops can be created.

This highly cultivated territory is watered by the Liao River, which enters Manchuria from Mongolia, 350 miles from its source, and flows into the sea near Newchwang. It is navigable at certain seasons for junks of varying size, as is also the Tai-szu Ho, its most important tributary, which joins it from the east. But the rivers have this peculiarity, that while in summer they supply a means of water transport, their surface becomes so strongly frozen over from November to March that they can be used for heavy traffic. The railway which leads southwards through Manchuria from Mukden to Port Arthur naturally avails itself of the level river - bed, and, like many another, coincides generally with the course of the stream.

The climate of Manchuria, temperate in summer, is in winter most severe. The rainy season occurs during the months of July and August, but its commencement and duration vary a good deal. Although the rainfall only amounts to about 13 inches throughout the year, at times it becomes so heavy as to inundate the country and cause damage to the railway.

Roads, as we know them, can hardly be said to exist at all. There are tracks across the rich soft soil, but after heavy rain, or when a thaw begins, they more nearly resemble impassable quagmires than anything else.

This lack of good communications limits the period during which military operations can be carried on to the summer months, because the cold in winter is so severe that troops are driven into winter quarters, and in the wet months, as has been shown, the transport is reduced to immobility. Winter quarters brought little comfort to the troops, and those they did occupy had largely to

be constructed by themselves ; for houses were so
sparse and widely scattered that it was difficult to
obtain accommodation in them.

Thus it will be seen that the nature of the
country restricted movements to a broad level plain
on either bank of a great river by no means favourable to strategical manœuvre, that the portion of
the year in which operations could be undertaken
at all was very considerably limited, and that,
owing to want of transport and to the absence
of communications, supplies had to be conveyed
chiefly by a single line of rail, supplemented by
river transport which coincided in its direction with
the line.

Obviously two armies meeting in such a region
were to a great extent restricted to attack and
defence up and down a line which they could not
leave, and were compelled by geographical conditions to operate on a front at right angles to
their main lines of communication. Wide turning
movements and vast strategical combinations, such
as Napoleon and Wellington conceived, were in the
circumstances impossible. The Russians removed
all their rolling stock as they fell back, while the
gauge of the line had to be altered before the
Japanese could utilize their own. The delays,
moreover, which the climate and other circumstances imposed on operations were aggravated by
the strategical situation, by which it was to the
interests of the Russians to delay offensive action
and await the attack of their enemy, and by
which, on the other hand, it was desirable for the
Japanese to put off decisive attack until the fall of

Port Arthur should have placed field forces in their full strength at the disposal of their generals.

In addition to this, of course, something is to be allowed for the somewhat inert if courageous characteristics of the Russian army, and something, too, to the ultra-methodical methods of their opponents, similarly coupled, though they were, with unexampled determination and bravery.

The resultant of all these influences and forces was that a campaign was fought in which attack and defence were conducted in a methodical and protracted manner, suggestive of the days of the Grande Monarque rather than that of our century. The part taken by the cavalry was very small, and no brilliant enterprises were carried through by them. The war tended to resemble siege operations more than anything else ; entrenchments, barbed wire, heavy cannon, night attacks, mines, even hand-grenades, the medieval properties of battle in close juxtaposition with the most scientific modern armaments, were much in evidence.

Experience derived from circumstances such as these must be received with caution if anything like a universal application is to be demanded for them. To wander into the question of how far the lessons are to be regarded as abnormal, and special, is a task far beyond the sphere of this book, but it becomes very legitimate and very necessary to point out that, amongst the influences which rendered the experiences of the Russo-Japanese War peculiar, those connected with geography are especially prominent.

CHAPTER XIII

CONCLUSION

In conclusion, we may ask ourselves, what lessons have we learnt from the preceding collection of geographical phenomena, and from the historical events that have been interwoven with them? To what do the recorded experiences of time point, and in what directions are the matters dealt with by geography likely to affect future strategy?

The study of geography in its broadest aspects most vividly appeals to us where the efforts made by human beings to minimize distances, surmount obstacles to intercourse, or substitute artificial restraints for natural obstructions to hostile movements, are illustrated. To bridge oceans, or abridge lonely illimitable wastes, to span great rivers, or tunnel through the roots of mountains, to filch territory from the sea, or lead the waves into channels through solid land—these are the stirring episodes, the most enduring monuments of human energy in the battle with Nature which has been going on ever since mankind emerged from a state of barbarism. To launch a boat at all was a victory over the limitations set by physical geography. To make paths over hills, or through

forests, was an encroachment on the arbitrary pro-
hibitions of the primeval universe. Step by step,
from one vantage-point to another, man fought his
way, till in his progress he came into contact with
yet other men struggling through natural obstacles
to greater comfort and greater freedom of action
in an opposite direction to his.

To pass from the Atlantic to the Pacific Ocean,
going from east to west, once the dream and effort
of a succession of lives, has now for several years
been an easy task by rail. A few days in a movable
hotel has replaced the doubling of Cape Horn.
More lately the railway has beaten the steamship
moving in a reverse direction, and Paris and
London are linked to Vladivostok by three weeks.
The traditions of the art of war are rudely disturbed by modern inventions appearing year by
year. The training of the soldier has advanced by
leaps and bounds since the time when he was
merely food for powder. Orders are written with
the classical correctness of a copy-book. Telephones and telegraph lines, or wireless systems, are
giving rest to puzzled despatch riders and foundered
horses. The implements of destruction have never
been so destructive, nor their efficiency so well
applied. As education spreads and scientific
methods develop, the most, no doubt, will be made
of every source of supply. The arts of healing and
of preventive sanitation keep pace with the most
bloodthirsty inventions for destroying life. We
are threatened with a recurrence of the age of
armour. It was James I. who said of that method
of protection that it was an excellent device, for it

not only prevented men being killed, but prevented their killing other men.   Alimentary, sanitary, and medical arrangements will no doubt in time attain such size and completeness that, as in the case of the knights in plate armour, movement will become difficult and manœuvre impossible, with the result that wars may end in a system of stalemate.   The millennium would then be in sight, yet is still a long way off.   But the hopes raised by the spread of civilization shrink again under the light of stricter examination.   Geography shows us how the expansive impulse of tribes and nations defy natural boundaries.   How, like the great forces of Nature by which were evolved the rivers and mountains and valleys of to-day, the ambitions of a growing race ultimately assert themselves, carry it over adjoining territories by a tidal flow, or, impatient at obstruction, make it burst upon them in an annihilating flood.   The energy of a nation is expressed in the growth of its population, because shooting machines cannot ultimately take the place of men, and Providence still favours the big battalions.   In these days of armed nations the petty standing armies of the pre-Napoleon period provoke derision.   Secure communications by sea once made British armies formidable on the Continent.   But then, compared to the relationship between them now, the Lilliputian armies of Continental monarchs only exceeded our stature by the thickness of a nail. Native vigour and independence of character were enough often to redress the balance.   Our forces were small, but not absurdly out of proportion to the other armies of European Powers.   The great

Frederick led only 22,000 Prussians to the memor-
able victory of Rossbach.   At Zorndorf he was at
the head of only 32,000 Prussians, at Hochkirch he
disposed of but 30,000 ; at Talavera the numbers on
either side were about 50,000.   But in the Crimea
the prestige and authority of our commanders were
already prejudiced by the smallness of the numbers
we were able to put into the field.   We ransacked
Europe to raise foreign contingents.   Germans and
Poles, temporarily enlisted, fought under our flag.
Since then we have dropped behind more and more.
We are ready, it is true, to send a larger expeditionary
force rapidly from our shores than we ever have
been, but even 160,000 men is a bagatelle when
measured by the standard of the Continental armies
of to-day.   Casualties to the number of 400,000
had to be replaced by the Germans in 1870, fighting
a victorious campaign in the richest country of the
world, with railways at their disposal and cantonments not difficult to find.   A year's war will exact
a toll from us, in casualties, of 70 per cent. of our
original strength, while the experiences reaped of
late in the Far East discredit the idea, which
prevailed until comparatively recent times, that
modern wars will be short and decisive.   To conquer the armed population of a country has ever
been accounted the most arduous and prolonged
task that can be set to a commander ; and war on
a large scale, in consequence of compulsory service,
now means nothing less than a struggle of whole
peoples.   The lesson that, in the long-run, the
numbers of the male population of a country must
make themselves felt, scarcely needs exposition.

Armaments are now of practically the same efficiency in all armies. Tactical formations and methods of handling troops do not so widely differ as to suggest that any marked advantage in that direction can promise success. The days when iron ramrods might turn the scale are over. Superior physique can be claimed no longer by any nation which does not put the best specimens of its manhood into the field. Genius no doubt will assert itself, and work wonders in the future as in the past, but no one knows where genius in war is to be discovered until the convulsions of the actual struggle fling it to the surface. What remains certain is that the vigour and numbers of a race will turn the scale, and that the forces some great powers can put into the fighting line are practically limited only by questions of supply. Alliances are little to be confided in. Ultimately Governments are governed by self-interest, as are men. An alliance that ceases to be an advantage, or even becomes a danger to one of the parties to a treaty, will not long be respected by that party. The growth of a country's population and of that of its colonies is to its fighting strength what the development of his stature and muscles and sinews are to the growing athlete. The future of the world is to those races who unite the inherent superiority of white men with the natural vitality, physique, and stolidity of the young barbarian. A race which does not grow, however intellectual, must ultimately succumb to those that show greater staying power in the struggle for life, because they have reservoirs of men behind them. No natural boundaries, no alliances, will hold back for long the nation that is pushed onward by the automatic forces of expansion. To attempt to prophesy is foolish. To gauge the outcome of all the factors—racial, political, physical, financial—that act and react on one another in determining the trend of future events, is impossible. Augury is defied while the Jews retain their special characteristics, and the Sultan still preserves his footing in Europe. But one branch of military, or, more properly speaking, of political geography, does register facts, and the facts may be interpreted by those who will adjust themselves to the task. Some will arrive at one conclusion, and some at another, or at any rate there will be various opinions, whether based on facts or not. But when prejudices are forgotten, when the growth of the population of England, of the Commonwealth, and of Canada is measured by the progress of colonization quoted in the case of Siberia, the deductions drawn will probably not widely differ where those who investigate them can lay claim to be impartial.

Looking back nearly a hundred years to the Congress of Vienna, we find that, in Europe, England, Spain, Portugal, Norway, and Sweden have alone retained the frontiers they then possessed. Holland and Belgium have become separate kingdoms, the German confederation has completely altered the situation in Central Europe, Greece has attained her long-cherished ambition, Italy is united, the Balkan Peninsula has been metamorphosed, and at the moment of writing further great changes are developing in that region. Great wars have been waged to end in stipulations and adjustments of territory and treaties, many of which are already obsolete. Racial tendencies are everywhere overtly or silently at work. National aspirations and schemes of aggrandizement are steadily pushed. Alliances are made and reconsidered on principles and bases that would sound strange to Castlereagh or even Palmerston. The neutrality of Belgium was formerly menaced by France, as the mouldering bastions of many a fortress testify, whereas Belgium now scents danger from quite an opposite direction. The stability of the European system depends on personalities and the duration of human life, rather than on any clearly recognized adjustment of power. And European interests alone no longer guide statesmen, the whole world is drawn into their purview, and affairs on the Pacific darken counsels that were already involved and intricate when only events on this side of the Atlantic were weighed.

Taking Europe alone into consideration, and leaving the problems of the rest of the globe on one side as too vast a subject to be further examined here, it is interesting to note how greatly the equilibrium of power has altered there since the beginning of the nineteenth century.

Italy, by the growth of her population and the development of her military resources, has since 1866 risen to the status of a great Power. The kingdom of Prussia may be said to have grown into the German Empire. The dominions of the Sultan have diminished more and more. The minor kingdoms of the Balkan Peninsula and Greece have sprung up. Norway and Sweden have fallen apart.

England, Spain, and Portugal alone have retained their ancient territorial limits.[1]

We may illustrate the transformation further by noting the remarks of the same author in his references to his own country:

" In 1700 the populations of the three great Powers, France, England, and the German Empire, numbered some 50,000,000. Of these 38 per cent. represented France.

" In 1789 the populations of the four great Powers (Russia now added to that category) numbered 96,000,000. Of these, 25 per cent. represented France.

" In 1815 the populations of the five great Powers (Prussia added) numbered about 139,000,000. Of these, 21 per cent. represented France.

" In 1872 the populations of the six great Powers (Italy added) numbered about 244,000,000. Of these, 14·8 per cent. represented France.

" In 1890 the populations of the six great Powers numbered about 298,000,000. Of these, 12·9 per cent. represented France."

A patriotic Frenchman thinks it right to call attention to the altered conditions in which a lack of expansion in her population has placed our neighbour and cordial friend. It were possible to pursue the subject further, and exhibit the relatively slow growth of the population of our own country and her colonies as a source of similar disquietude, when the immense growth of our responsibilities all over the globe, and the altered

---

[1] *Resumé de Géographie physique et historique*, by Colonel Niox, the second edition of which was published in Paris by Librairie Ch. Delagrave in 1900.

stategical situation brought about by the development of other nations far distant from our shores,
are considered.   To do so, however, scarcely falls
within the sphere with which these pages deal.
The facts are sufficiently obvious, and are already
a cause of anxiety to many Britons.   That a
remedy may be forthcoming must be the aspiration
of all.   The fringe only of a great subject has been
touched in these pages, but the limits of Europe
and its politics and geography have been left far
behind, even though but a comparatively narrow
portion of the world beyond our immediate knowledge has been traversed.

" What the Swede intends and what the French "
have long ceased to be considered together.   But
until comparatively recent dates European politics
were enough to occupy the thoughts of our statesmen, even if a century and a half ago American
affairs were sufficiently pressing to call forth the
highest eloquence and energy of our greatest men.
However possible, if foolish, it was then to forget the
world in thinking only of England and Europe, to
do so has become wholly impossible now.

It is the distant parts of the earth that will, in
all human probability, call forth the greatest dis-
plays of energy, and the problems that will have
to be solved by us are likely to be connected just
as much with the progress of nations and events
on the Pacific seaboards as those of which more
is heard nearer home.   An appreciation of the
military geography of Siberia, Central Asia,
and Manchuria seems now at least as necessary
as the knowledge of rivers and mountain-ranges

and frontiers of the Continent; for a lesson that military geography emphasizes is that East and West are becoming every day more closely bound together, and that when equilibrium is upset in one hemisphere oscillations and disturbances will occur in the other. In both hemispheres the expansion and resultant resistance of great races forging on in certain directions to attain a national aspiration or need, opposing others or seeking union with one another, will sooner or later engender friction, heat, and war.

Even if we could become isolated as regards Europe, we could never become so as regards the world. We must, if we desire to maintain our position all over the world, be of the world, and understand the causes and origin of the commotions that have disturbed the world, and will again disturb it. Military geography in its broad aspect supplies some at least of the knowledge that is essential to an understanding of these causes, and therefore we should study it not only for the sake of acquiring certain empirical information, but because it helps us on our way towards enlightenment in a sphere beyond the record of mere facts.

APPENDIX I

CONVENTION BETWEEN THE UNITED KINGDOM
AND RUSSIA RELATING TO PERSIA, AFGHANISTAN, AND
THIBET.[1]

SIGNED AT ST. PETERSBURGH, AUGUST 31, 1907.

[*Ratifications exchanged at St. Petersburgh, September 23, 1907.*]

CONVENTION.

HIS MAJESTY the King of the United Kingdom of Great Britain and Ireland and of the British Dominions beyond the Seas, Emperor of India, and His Majesty the Emperor of All the Russias, animated by the sincere desire to settle by mutual agreement different questions concerning the interests of their States on the Continent of Asia, have determined to conclude Agreements destined to prevent all cause of misunderstanding between Great Britain and Russia in regard to the questions referred to, and have nominated for this purpose their respective Plenipotentiaries, to wit:

His Majesty the King of the United Kingdom of Great Britain and Ireland and of the British Dominions beyond the Seas, Emperor of India, the Right Honourable Sir Arthur Nicolson, His Majesty's Ambassador Extraordinary and Plenipotentiary to His Majesty the Emperor of All the Russias;

His Majesty the Emperor of All the Russias, the Master

[1] Extracted from "Treaty Series, No. 34." London, Harrison and Sons. Price 1d.

17—2

of his Court, Alexander Iswolsky, Minister for Foreign Affairs ;

Who, having communicated to each other their full powers, found in good and due form, have agreed on the following :

AGREEMENT CONCERNING PERSIA.

The Governments of Great Britain and Russia having mutually engaged to respect the integrity and independence of Persia, and sincerely desiring the preservation of order throughout that country and its peaceful development, as well as the permanent establishment of equal advantages for the trade and industry of all other nations ;

Considering that each of them has, for geographical and economic reasons, a special interest in the maintenance of peace and order in certain provinces of Persia adjoining, or in the neighbourhood of, the Russian frontier on the one hand, and the frontiers of Afghanistan and Baluchistan on the other hand ; and being desirous of avoiding all cause of conflict between their respective interests in the above-mentioned provinces of Persia ;

Have agreed on the following terms :

I.

Great Britain engages not to seek for herself, and not to support in favour of British subjects, or in favour of the subjects of third Powers, any Concessions of a political or commercial nature—such as Concessions for railways, banks, telegraphs, roads, transport, insurance, etc.—beyond a line starting from Kasr-i-Shirin, passing through Isfahan, Yezd, Kakhk, and ending at a point on the Persian frontier at the intersection of the Russian and Afghan frontiers, and not to oppose, directly or indirectly, demands for similar Concessions in this region which are supported by the Russian Government. It is understood that the above-mentioned places are included in the region in which Great Britain engages not to seek the Concessions referred to.

II.

Russia, on her part, engages not to seek for herself and not to support, in favour of Russian subjects, or in favour of the subjects of third Powers, any Concessions of a political or commercial nature—such as Concessions for railways, banks, telegraphs, roads, transport, insurance, etc.—beyond a line going from the Afghan frontier by way of Gazik, Birjand, Kerman, and ending at Bunder Abbas, and not to oppose, directly or indirectly, demands for similar Concessions in this region which are supported by the British Government. It is understood that the above-mentioned places are included in the region in which Russia engages not to seek the Concessions referred to.

III.

Russia, on her part, engages not to oppose, without previous arrangement with Great Britain, the grant of any Concessions whatever to British subjects in the regions of Persia situated between the lines mentioned in Articles I. and II.

Great Britain undertakes a similar engagement as regards the grants of Concessions to Russian subjects in the same regions of Persia.

All Concessions existing at present in the regions indicated in Articles I. and II. are maintained.

IV.

It is understood that the revenues of all the Persian customs, with the exception of those of Farsistan and of the Persian Gulf, revenues guaranteeing the amortization and the interest of the loans concluded by the Government of the Shah with the " Banque d'Escompte et des Prêts de Perse " up to the date of the signature of the present Agreement, shall be devoted to the same purpose as in the past.

It is equally understood that the revenues of the Persian customs of Farsistan and of the Persian Gulf, as well as those of the fisheries on the Persian shore of the Caspian

Sea and those of the Posts and Telegraphs, shall be devoted, as in the past, to the service of the loans concluded by the Government of the Shah with the Imperial Bank of Persia up to the date of the signature of the present Agreement.

v.

In the event of irregularities occurring in the amortization or the payment of the interest of the Persian loans concluded with the " Banque d'Escompte et des Prêts de Perse " and with the Imperial Bank of Persia up to the date of the signature of the present Agreement, and in the event of the necessity arising for Russia to establish control over the sources of revenue guaranteeing the regular service of the loans concluded with the first-named bank, and situated in the region mentioned in Article II. of the present Agreement, or for Great Britain to establish control over the sources of revenue guaranteeing the regular service of the loans concluded with the second-named bank, and situated in the region mentioned in Article I. of the present Agreement, the British and Russian Governments undertake to enter beforehand into a friendly exchange of ideas with a view to determine, in agreement with each other, the measures of control in question, and to avoid all interference which would not be in conformity with the principles governing the present Agreement.

CONVENTION CONCERNING AFGHANISTAN.

The High Contracting Parties, in order to insure perfect security on their respective frontiers in Central Asia, and to maintain in these regions a solid and lasting peace, have concluded the following Convention :

ARTICLE I.

His Britannic Majesty's Government declare that they have no intention of changing the political status of Afghanistan.

His Britannic Majesty's Government further engage to

exercise their influence in Afghanistan only in a pacific sense, and they will not themselves take, nor encourage Afghanistan to take, any measures threatening Russia.

The Russian Government, on their part, declare that they recognize Afghanistan as outside the sphere of Russian influence, and they engage that all their political relations with Afghanistan shall be conducted through the inter- mediary of His Britannic Majesty's Government; they further engage not to send any Agents into Afghanistan.

ARTICLE II.

The Government of His Britannic Majesty having declared in the Treaty signed at Kabul on the 21st March, 1905, that they recognize the Agreement and the engagements con- cluded with the late Ameer Abdur Rahman, and that they have no intention of interfering in the internal government of Afghan territory, Great Britain engages neither to annex nor to occupy in contravention of that Treaty any portion of Afghanistan, or to interfere in the internal administration of the country, provided that the Ameer fulfils the engage- ments already contracted by him towards His Britannic Majesty's Government under the above-mentioned Treaty.

ARTICLE III.

The Russian and Afghan authorities, specially designated for the purpose on the frontier or in the frontier provinces, may establish direct relations with each other for the settle- ment of local questions of a non-political character.

ARTICLE IV.

His Britannic Majesty's Government and the Russian Government affirm their adherence to the principle of equality of commercial opportunity in Afghanistan, and they agree that any facilities which may have been, or shall be hereafter, obtained for British and British-Indian trade and traders, shall be equally enjoyed by Russian trade and traders. Should the progress of trade establish the necessity for Commercial Agents, the two Governments will agree as to what measures shall be taken, due regard, of course, being had to the Ameer's sovereign rights.

ARTICLE V.

The present arrangements will only come into force when His Britannic Majesty's Government shall have notified to the Russian Government the consent of the Ameer to the terms stipulated above.

AGREEMENT CONCERNING THIBET.

The Governments of Great Britain and Russia recognizing the suzerain rights of China in Thibet, and considering the fact that Great Britain, by reason of her geographical position, has a special interest in the maintenance of the *status quo* in the external relations of Thibet, have made the following Agreement :

ARTICLE I.

The two High Contracting Parties engage to respect the territorial integrity of Thibet and to abstain from all interference in its internal administration.

ARTICLE II.

In conformity with the admitted principle of the suzerainty of China over Thibet, Great Britain and Russia engage not to enter into negotiations with Thibet except through the intermediary of the Chinese Government. This engagement does not exclude the direct relations between British Commercial Agents and the Thibetan authorities provided for in Article V. of the Convention between Great Britain and Thibet of the 7th September, 1904, and confirmed by the Convention between Great Britain and China of the 27th April, 1906 ; nor does it modify the engagements entered into by Great Britain and China in Article I. of the said Convention of 1906.

It is clearly understood that Buddhists, subjects of Great Britain or of Russia, may enter into direct relations on strictly religious matters with the Dalai Lama and the other representatives of Buddhism in Thibet ; the Governments of Great Britain and Russia engage, so far as they are concerned, not to allow those relations to infringe the stipulations of the present Agreement.

ARTICLE III.

The British and Russian Governments respectively engage not to send Representatives to Lhassa.

ARTICLE IV.

The two High Contracting Parties engage neither to seek nor to obtain, whether for themselves or their subjects, any Concessions for railways, roads, telegraphs, and mines, or other rights in Thibet.

ARTICLE V.

The two Governments agree that no part of the revenues of Thibet, whether in kind or in cash, shall be pledged or assigned to Great Britain or Russia or to any of their subjects.

Annex to the Agreement between Great Britain and Russia concerning Thibet.

Great Britain reaffirms the Declaration, signed by his Excellency the Viceroy and Governor-General of India, and appended to the ratification of the Convention of the 7th September, 1904, to the effect that the occupation of the Chumbi Valley by British forces shall cease after the payment of three annual instalments of the indemnity of 25,00,000 rupees, provided that the trade marts mentioned in Article II. of that Convention have been effectively opened for three years, and that in the meantime the Thibetan authorities have faithfully complied in all respects with the terms of the said Convention of 1904. It is clearly understood that if the occupation of the Chumbi Valley by the British forces has, for any reason, not been terminated at the time anticipated in the above Declaration, the British and Russian Governments will enter upon a friendly exchange of views on this subject.

The present Convention shall be ratified, and the ratifications exchanged at St. Petersburgh as soon as possible.

In witness whereof the respective Plenipotentiaries have signed the present Convention and affixed thereto their seals.

Done in duplicate at St. Petersburgh, the 18th (31st) August, 1907.

(L.S.)   A. NICOLSON.
(L.S.)   ISWOLSKY.

ANNEXES.

ST. PETERSBURGH,
August 18 (31), 1907.

M. LE MINISTRE,

With reference to the Agreement regarding Thibet, signed to-day, I have the honour to make the following Declaration to your Excellency :

" His Britannic Majesty's Government think it desirable, so far as they are concerned, not to allow, unless by a previous agreement with the Russian Government, for a period of three years from the date of the present communication, the entry into Thibet of any scientific mission whatever, on condition that a like assurance is given on the part of the Imperial Russian Government.

" His Britannic Majesty's Government propose, moreover, to approach the Chinese Government with a view to induce them to accept a similar obligation for a corresponding period ; the Russian Government will, as a matter of course, take similar action.

" At the expiration of the term of three years above mentioned His Britannic Majesty's Government will, if necessary, consult with the Russian Government as to the desirability of any ulterior measures with regard to scientific expeditions to Thibet."

I avail, etc.,
(Signed)   A. NICOLSON.

St. Petersburgh,
August 18 (31), 1907.

M. L'Ambassadeur,

In reply to your Excellency's note of to-day's date, I have the honour to declare that the Imperial Russian Government think it desirable, so far as they are concerned, not to allow, unless by a previous agreement with the British Government, for a period of three years from the date of the present communication, the entry into Thibet of any scientific mission whatever.

Like the British Government, the Imperial Government propose to approach the Chinese Government with a view to induce them to accept a similar obligation for a corresponding period.

It is understood that at the expiration of the term of three years the two Governments will, if necessary, consult with each other as to the desirability of any ulterior measures with regard to scientific expeditions to Thibet.

Accept, etc.,

(Signed)   Iswolsky.

APPENDIX II

THE NEW ANGLO-JAPANESE AGREEMENT.

From the "Times" of September 27, 1905.

THE following "Despatch to His Majesty's Ambassador at St. Petersburgh, forwarding a copy of the Agreement between the United Kingdom and Japan, signed at London, August 12, 1905," was issued yesterday as a Parliamentary paper [Cd. 2690]:

THE MARQUESS OF LANSDOWNE TO SIR C. HARDINGE.*

FOREIGN OFFICE,
September 6, 1905.

SIR,
          I inclose, for your Excellency's information, a copy of a new Agreement concluded between His Majesty's Government and that of Japan in substitution for that of January 30, 1902. You will take an early opportunity of communicating the new Agreement to the Russian Government.

It was signed on August 12, and you will explain that it would have been immediately made public but for the fact that negotiations had at that time already commenced between Russia and Japan, and that the publication of such a document whilst those negotiations were still in progress would obviously have been improper and inopportune.

The Russian Government will, I trust, recognize that the new Agreement is an international instrument to which no exception can be taken by any of the Powers interested in

* A similar despatch was addressed to His Majesty's ambassador at Paris.

the affairs of the Far East. You should call special attention to the objects mentioned in the preamble as those by which the policy of the Contracting Parties is inspired. His Majesty's Government believe that they may count upon the good-will and support of all the Powers in endeavouring to maintain peace in Eastern Asia, and in seeking to uphold the integrity and independence of the Chinese Empire and the principle of equal opportunities for the commerce and industry of all nations in that country.

On the other hand, the special interests of the Contracting Parties are of a kind upon which they are fully entitled to insist, and the announcement that those interests must be safeguarded is one which can create no surprise, and need give rise to no misgivings.

I call your especial attention to the wording of Article II., which lays down distinctly that it is only in the case of an unprovoked attack made on one of the Contracting Parties by another Power or Powers, and when that Party is defending its territorial rights and special interests from aggressive action, that the other Party is bound to come to its assistance.

Article III., dealing with the question of Corea, is deserving of especial attention. It recognizes in the clearest terms the paramount position which Japan at this moment occupies, and must henceforth occupy, in Corea, and her right to take any measures which she may find necessary for the protection of her political, military, and economic interests in that country. It is, however, expressly provided that such measures must not be contrary to the principle of equal opportunities for the commerce and industry of other nations. The new Treaty no doubt differs at this point conspicuously from that of 1902. It has, however, become evident that Corea, owing to its close proximity to the Japanese Empire and its inability to stand alone, must fall under the control and tutelage of Japan.

His Majesty's Government observe with satisfaction that this point was readily conceded by Russia in the Treaty of Peace recently concluded with Japan, and they have every reason to believe that similar views are held by other Powers with regard to the relations which should subsist between Japan and Corea.

His Majesty's Government venture to anticipate that the alliance thus concluded, designed as it is with objects which are purely peaceful and for the protection of rights and interests the validity of which cannot be contested, will be regarded with approval by the Government to which you are accredited. They are justified in believing that its conclusion may not have been without effect in facilitating the settlement by which the war has been so happily brought to an end, and they earnestly trust that it may, for many years to come, be instrumental in securing the peace of the world in those regions which come within its scope.

I am, etc.,
(Signed)   LANSDOWNE.

Inclosure.

AGREEMENT BETWEEN THE UNITED KINGDOM AND JAPAN, SIGNED AT LONDON, AUGUST 12, 1905.

PREAMBLE.

The Governments of Great Britain and Japan, being desirous of replacing the Agreement concluded between them on January 30, 1902, by fresh stipulations, have agreed upon the following Articles, which have for their object:

(*a*) The consolidation and maintenance of the general peace in the regions of Eastern Asia and of India;

(*b*) The preservation of the common interests of all Powers in China by insuring the independence and integrity of the Chinese Empire and the principle of equal opportunities for the commerce and industry of all nations in China;

(*c*) The maintenance of the territorial rights of the High Contracting Parties in the regions of Eastern Asia and of

India, and the defence of their special interests in the said regions :

ARTICLE I.

It is agreed that whenever, in the opinion of either Great Britain or Japan, any of the rights and interests referred to in the preamble of this Agreement are in jeopardy, the two Governments will communicate with one another fully and frankly, and will consider in common the measures which should be taken to safeguard those menaced rights or interests.

ARTICLE II.

If by reason of unprovoked attack or aggressive action, wherever arising, on the part of any other Power or Powers, either Contracting Party should be involved in war in defence of its territorial rights or special interests mentioned in the preamble of this Agreement, the other Contracting Party will at once come to the assistance of its ally, and will conduct the war in common, and make peace in mutual agreement with it.

ARTICLE III.

Japan possessing paramount political, military, and economic interests in Corea, Great Britain recognizes the right of Japan to take such measures of guidance, control, and protection in Corea as she may deem proper and necessary to safeguard and advance those interests, provided always that such measures are not contrary to the principle of equal opportunities for the commerce and industry of all nations.

ARTICLE IV.

Great Britain having a special interest in all that concerns the security of the Indian frontier, Japan recognizes her right to take such measures in the proximity of that frontier as she may find necessary for safeguarding her Indian possessions.

ARTICLE V.

The High Contracting Parties agree that neither of them will, without consulting the other, enter into separate arrangements with another Power to the prejudice of the objects described in the preamble of this Agreement.

ARTICLE VI.

As regards the present war between Japan and Russia, Great Britain will continue to maintain strict neutrality unless some other Power or Powers should join in hostilities against Japan, in which case Great Britain will come to the assistance of Japan, and will conduct the war in common, and make peace in mutual agreement with Japan.

ARTICLE VII.

The conditions under which armed assistance shall be afforded by either Power to the other in the circumstances mentioned in the present Agreement, and the means by which such assistance is to be made available, will be arranged by the Naval and Military authorities of the Contracting Parties, who will from time to time consult one another fully and freely upon all questions of mutual interest.

ARTICLE VIII.

The present Agreement shall, subject to the provisions of Article VI., come into effect immediately after the date of its signature, and remain in force for ten years from that date.

In case neither of the High Contracting Parties should have notified twelve months before the expiration of the said ten years the intention of terminating it, it shall remain binding until the expiration of one year from the day on which either of the High Contracting Parties shall have denounced it. But if, when the date fixed for its expiration arrives, either ally is actually engaged in war, the alliance shall, *ipso facto*, continue until peace is concluded.

In faith whereof the Undersigned, duly authorized by their respective Governments, have signed this Agreement and have affixed thereto their Seals.

Done in duplicate at London, the 12th day of August, 1905.

(L.S.)   LANSDOWNE,
His Britannic Majesty's Principal Secretary
of State for Foreign Affairs.

(L.S.)   TADASU HAYASHI,
Envoy Extraordinary and Minister Plenipo-
tentiary of His Majesty the Emperor of
Japan at the Court of St. James.

APPENDIX III

A UNIQUE ACHIEVEMENT OF CAVALRY AND HORSE ARTILLERY, RENDERED POSSIBLE BY CLIMATIC CONDITIONS IN 1795.

THE following account of the incident referred to on p. 76 is so extraordinary that it has been given in extenso. Denison says : " To the French cavalry belongs the credit of having been the only cavalry that ever captured a fleet of warships on the sea."

" Un fait, d'une nature toute nouvelle et unique, signale la fin de cette expédition [*i.e.*, the French invasion of Holland in 1795]. Comme 14 vaisseaux de guerre hollandais arrêtés par les glaces, près du Texel, auraient pu être emmenés par les Anglais, si le dégal était survenu, Pichegru prescrivit immédiatement de s'en saisir en employant les premières troupes disponibles. Le 22 janvier, le général Devoynter fut chargé d'aller sommer ces vaisseaux. À cet effet, il se mit en route dans la nuit avec le 3e bataillon de Chasseurs-Tirailleurs, un détachement de 120 chevaux du 3e Hussards et 2 escouades d'Artillerie à cheval. Les pieds des chevaux furent enveloppés d'étoupe. Les Hussards purent donc s'élancer sur la glace et venir sommer la flotte, qui se rendit."

[Picard (Comdt. L.), " La Cavalerie dans les guerres de la Révolution et de l'Empire," i., p. 86.]

THE END